A SWING FOR LIFE

A SWING FOR LIFE

NICK FALDO

WITH RICHARD SIMMONS

REVISED & UPDATED

SIMON &
SCHUSTER

You will find tags (like the one shown above) throughout this book, and you can use them to access enhanced digital content. To do so, simply download the free app at gettag.mobi. Then hold your phone's camera a few inches away from the tag and enjoy what comes next.

If you access video content through a mobile device, message and data rates may apply.

This edition published in Great Britain by Simon & Schuster UK Ltd, 2012
A CBS COMPANY

1 3 5 7 9 10 8 6 4 2

Simon & Schuster UK Ltd
1st Floor
222 Gray's Inn Road
London
WC1X 8HB

www.simonandschuster.co.uk

Simon & Schuster Australia
Sydney

Simon & Schuster India,
New Delhi

Designed by Tim Oliver

Archival photographs provided by Getty Images; photo sequence on page 15 courtesy of Peter Dazely

Manufactured in China

A CIP catalogue for this book is available
from the British Library.

Hardback ISBN 978-1-47110-260-8

To Mum, Dad, and the kids

CONTENTS

INTRODUCTION   ix

ONE   MY KEY THOUGHTS (AND ABSOLUTE *MUSTS*)   1

TWO   THE FUNDAMENTALS   13

THREE   BUILDING A SWING FOR LIFE   33

FOUR   TIMING AND TEMPO   77

FIVE   WORKING THE BALL   99

SIX   A DRIVING LESSON   117

SEVEN   PUTTING—THE PERSONAL TOUCH   149

EIGHT   CHIPPING AND PITCHING—MY SHORT-GAME SYSTEM   183

NINE   LEARN TO LOVE THE SAND   215

TEN   PLAYING THE GAME   243

ACKNOWLEDGMENTS   270

VIDEO LESSON TABLE OF CONTENTS   273

TOURNAMENT VICTORIES   274

OR SOMEONE who loves the game of golf as much as I do, the opportunity to extend a playing career beyond the ropes and into the world of television has been a dream come true. I may not be hitting all the shots out on tour these days, but I do at least get to call them alongside my colleagues at CBS Sports and Golf Channel, a privileged day job that comes with a front-row seat from which to study and analyze the new generation of international stars.

The depth of talent in professional golf today is quite astonishing. And what strikes me most when I walk along a range is the quality and consistency of the fundamentals with which these young players are working. There's no real mystery behind the standard of scoring that we see week in and week out—at the highest level the players who make the game look easy are doing so with techniques based on a sound appreciation of golf's most rudimentary lessons and values. (Not to mention phenomenal putting skills.) You just don't see a world-class player with a crooked grip, a lazy posture, or skewed alignment. These details are fine-tuned on a daily basis as ever-more-athletic players work on the quality of their body action and "core" speed—the modern parlance for the rotary motion

THE MAJOR BREAKTHROUGH:
Grinding out 18 straight pars on Sunday, Nick Faldo won the first of his three Open Championships at Muirfield, Scotland, in 1987.

that lies at the heart of every solid, *repeating* swing.

I'm well aware that for the golfer sitting at home, the only conclusion to draw from the sea of red numbers posted on the leaderboard is that these guys are on another planet, talking a different language and playing the game based on some secret and superior set of operating instructions. This is where I dive in—with a reality check! In the role of analyst, and backed up by those incredible slow-motion sequences that are such a popular feature of TV coverage, I have the opportunity to add a sense of perspective, to help the viewer understand the swing and recognize the key techniques that can help his or her game. There is nothing I enjoy more than stripping away this veneer of mystique to reveal that even at the highest level, golf is all about the respect a player has for the fundamentals—the lessons that have stood the test of time. Drawing on the knowledge that I accumulated in my own career, I am going to make sure that's precisely the message that comes across in this book.

GOLF HAS BEEN my life and passion now for more than 40 years. And though my playing appearances these days are few and far between, I still love nothing more than to get out to the range and lose myself for a couple of hours just hitting balls—tinkering, tweaking, experimenting, and fine-tuning. I'm forever *learning*. Practicing alone with your thoughts is one of golf's most

satisfying pleasures, and in the process of updating my notes and getting my swing into shape for the video and photo shoots supporting this project, it occurred to me that the more I've learned about this game, the simpler I've made it. Exploring that notion further, I found myself asking some very basic questions as I worked my way through every shot in the bag: *What are the pri-*

CALLING THE SHOTS: Shy and retiring? The opportunity to join Jim Nantz and the team at CBS Television has provided the six-time major champion with the platform to share his knowledge and experience with golf fans around the world.

orities I have to focus on to make a solid, repeating swing? What are the absolute musts *I need to satisfy in order to experience the feelings and sensations that I have always associated with playing good golf? What binds together the related skills of chipping and pitching that are so vital to consistently good scoring?* Time and again my conclusions brought me back to a checklist of thoughts and phrases that I recognize as the underlying score to a game that's rooted in the quality of the fundamentals—the very same lessons I observe on tour. The inescapable *musts* I now want to share with you.

Published to celebrate the 25th

anniversary of my first major victory, the 1987 Open Championship at Muirfield, this new and updated edition of the original *A Swing for Life* represents the ultimate collection of swing thoughts, observations, and discoveries that I have made in a lifetime dedicated to the game. This is not a book that deals too much with theory or elaborate explanations, but one that provides a practical, down-to-earth account of the way I believe a good swing takes shape. In moving through the fundamentals, developing the concept of the "body-controlled" swing, and dealing with all aspects of the short game and putting, I have tried to phrase each of the lessons just as I would if you were beside me on the range. Along the way, you will find my ideas supported with many of the drills I've used in my own tournament preparation—valuable shortcuts that will introduce you to moves and sensations that I know will lead to better and more consistent golf.

Asked to share his swing secrets, Ben Hogan famously replied that he found "the answers in the dirt," and in that same vein I can put up my hand and say that I've hit enough balls to know what works and what doesn't. I know

exactly what it takes to make a swing change and how valuable certain practice routines can be in the process of integrating new thoughts and feelings. More than that, I can tell you with absolute certainty that the "body-controlled" philosophy upon which I built a swing capable of winning major championships

will provide you with a lifetime's enjoyment as you prepare to embark on your own journey of enlightenment and discovery. I'm fine-tuning the details of that swing to this day—and that's the beauty of the concept you

 POINT YOUR SMART-PHONE'S CAMERA AT IT AND ENJOY THE VIDEO.

The lessons featured in this book have been tried and tested over decades, but we're pleased to include a cutting-edge method that allows you to enjoy them on demand in video format. In each chapter, you will see a Microsoft Tag. When you scan these Tags with your smartphone, you will be taken directly to a video of Nick Faldo giving a demonstration of one of the lessons detailed within that section of the book. These videos make the reading experience more dynamic.

will find running through every single chapter in this book. With a clear visual imprint of the natural athletic motion found in the swing (a logical chain of events that *always* has its origins in the setup position), you will find the lasting inspiration to simplify and improve the skills that comprise a solid game of golf.

A **FINAL WORD BEFORE** we head out to the practice tee. I played my best golf when my hands, arms, and shoulders felt "syrupy," a sensation that came directly from the grip. Down the years, a lot of golfers have misunderstood the "body-controlled" swing as one in which the hands are "quiet" or passive, a notion I am going to put to rest. The ability to swing every club in the bag with the same unhurried rhythm was one of my greatest assets, and I like to think that anyone who saw me play at the height of my career appreciated not only the quality and resilience of my swing but also the artistry at the heart of its making. My game was built around the security of a bulletproof body action within which my hands and forearms were very much "alive" to the business of swinging the clubhead. *Feel within a framework*—that was the secret to my success. And that's what I'm going to teach you.

Enjoy the game.

—*Sir Nick Faldo*

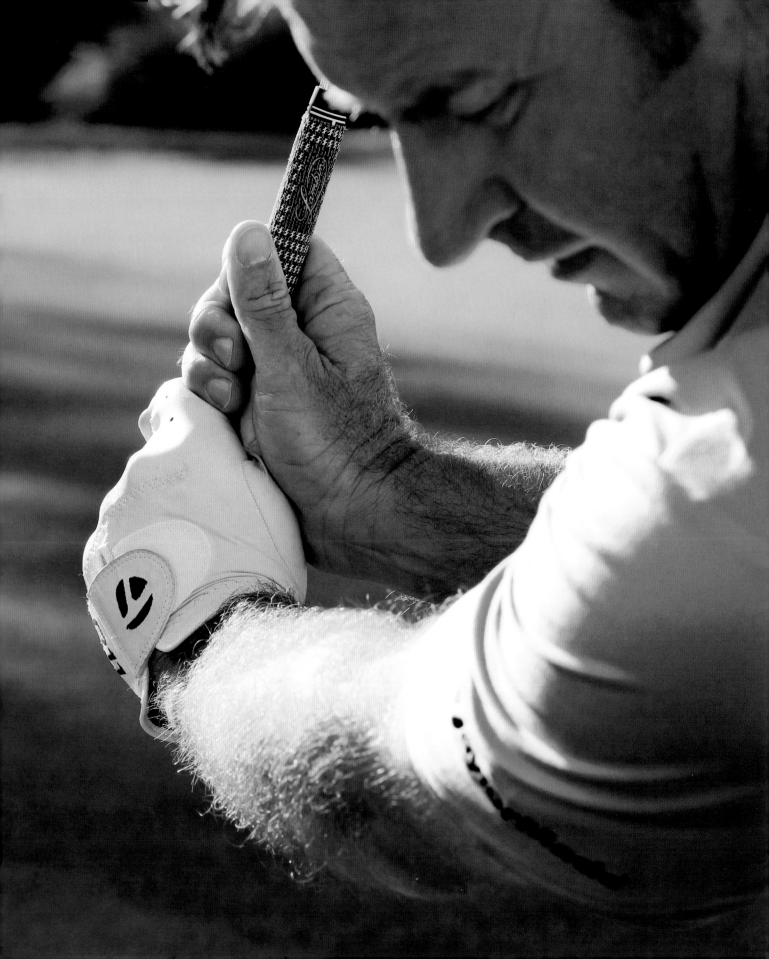

CHAPTER

MY KEY THOUGHTS (AND ABSOLUTE *MUSTS*)

THE SIMPLE CUES AND PHRASES THAT
I RELY ON TO KEEP MY SWING TICKING
OVER CAN HELP YOU CONCEPTUALIZE
A MOVEMENT IN WHICH YOUR HANDS
AND ARMS SWING IN HARMONY WITH
THE ROTATION OF YOUR BODY. **ALL
YOU NEED IS A "READY" SETUP**
THAT WILL INSPIRE A CHAIN REACTION
OF COORDINATED MOTION.

LIKE EVERY other athletic movement, a good golf swing engages the whole body in a sequence that relies on simple laws of physics to generate energy and speed. There's a distinct rhythm and a sense of "togetherness" as the arms and hands flow with the winding and un-winding of the torso; just like a coiled spring, the bigger muscles in the up-per body rotate over the resistance of the knees and hips, while the feet interact with the ground for a con-trolled and balanced weight shift, back and through.

These are the notions we're about to explore in the process of building a natural swing—one firmly based around the structure of a solid setup position. I men-tioned in my introduction that the more I've learned about this game, the simpler I've made it, and my "lightbulb moment" oc-curred when I began to appreciate the way in which a sound, rotary body action inspires (and indeed governs) a logical chain of events as the hands and arms respond to that momentum.

"The dog wags the tail" was how my coach, David Leadbetter, used to describe the philosophy, and as a result of our collabora-tion, the renaissance of my career was built around a body action that never let me down. Tee to green, I worked on honing the details of the setup position so that my body's movement could then control the show. You have this to discover: The better your body works, the more easily you establish good tempo and the more efficiently you will repeat a solid swing. Better still, within the security of that framework, your hands and forearms can enjoy the freedom to *play golf*.

Look around at other sports, and you can identify plenty of examples in which energy gener-ated by the rotation of the body is translated into speed: the baseball pitcher coiling for a fastball; the discus thrower using centrifugal

force; a tennis player winding up for a big serve. A good golf swing shares the same athleticism and body dynamic, but the challenge in this game is being able to synchronize the movement of the arms and hands to the heartbeat of that body action. During my hiatus in the mid-1980s, I focused most of my energy on the range, specifically rehearsing drills that helped me blend my arm swing with my body rotation so that I created a chain reaction. While out hitting balls, I would condense swing thoughts into simple "keys" to help me focus on the moves and feelings that I was looking to repeat—a habit that would prove invaluable under tournament pressure during the best years of my career.

"My Key Thoughts" remains one of my favorite chapters in the

THE SWING THOUGHTS **I relied on to win six major championships keep my swing ticking over to this day.**

original *A Swing for Life* for the way in which the six-part sequence captures not only the logic but also the rhythm of a solid, repeating swing. Of course, specific swing thoughts come and go, but these are typical of the cues and phrases I've relied on to reproduce my swing under the pressure of major championship golf, and in that context they offer a glimpse of just how uncomplicated your thinking needs to be as you prepare to find your true *swing*. They have stood the test of time, too. Seventeen years since the publication of the original book, these Key Thoughts and *musts* enable me to stand on a range and feel a freedom and a rhythm that allows me to hit solid golf shots.

As you work through the book and find out more about the way a good swing works, certain words and phrases will strike a chord in your own mind, and you'll use these to inspire your own chain reaction. Make a note of them. Write them in your yardage book or on the palm of your glove. Simple thoughts are easy to grasp; better still, they are easy to *repeat*.

VIDEO LESSON: SWING OVERVIEW **The whole in one: Nick Faldo condenses his philosophy on the golf swing into a simple series of images that will help you to conceptualize a solid and fluent motion.**

AT THE SETUP

KNEES

WITH MY WEIGHT on the balls of my feet, my all-time number-one swing thought—*knees*—reminds me to flex and brace the knees until I feel a strong athletic tension in each thigh. This is an absolute *must!* As you bend from the hips to create a distinct spine angle, this simple cue sharpens up your posture generally and helps you engage and stabilize your body core in readiness to make a dynamic swing. As the arms hang freely from the shoulders, a moderate-to-firm (but always sensitive) grip pressure keeps the wrists and forearms "alive" to the weight of the clubhead. You need to feel that weight on the end of the shaft to be able to *swing* it.

Once I'm ready to play, I waggle the clubhead to prime the wrist-and-forearm rotation that I'm looking for at the start of the swing, a final trigger that not only peps up the whole body in readiness for action but also establishes a sense of the rhythm to come.

By the time you get to the end of this book, you're going to be tired of hearing me say this, but the role of the knees is crucial in the process of maintaining athletic posture. At the setup, remind yourself of that "springy" sensation on the balls of your feet as often as you can; in doing so, you will recognize the importance of the muscles in the rear end that help you stabilize your body core and thus enjoy a more consistent rotation of the torso around the axis of your spine angle.

THE FIRST MOVES
TURN, ROTATE, AND SET

FOR ME, THERE is no better feeling than that of the clubhead swinging and gathering pace early in the backswing with a synchronized arm, wrist, and body action. Everything is linked together. This was a particularly effective thought for me at Muirfield during the 1992 Open, where my swing really did gel over all four days of the Championship. The key is the *timing* of the movement of your hands and arms with the rotation of your body right from the word "go." Setting off that coordinated motion (and capitalizing on the sensation of a good waggle), I focus on gently rotating my left forearm in a clockwise direction as my arms swing in harmony with my body motion. The hands, forearms, and stomach work *together* to create positive early momentum you can build on. From here, all I have to concentrate on is turning the bigger muscles in my upper body over the foundation—and indeed resistance—of my hips and knees. As I refined my swing over the years, this checkpoint became a favorite, the swing cue *turn, rotate, and set* reinforcing my desire to *turn* my upper body and belly, *rotate* the left forearm, and *set* the wrists up in the process of swinging the clubhead through the security of this halfway checkpoint. (In fact, a great range drill is to take a short iron and hit balls as you say the words "rotate and set" out loud not only in time with a three-quarter backswing but again into the follow-through, looking to mirror that position as you watch the flight of the ball. This is great for rhythm, too.)

TO THE TOP
TURN AND *COMPLETE*

. . . AND HERE'S the proof. As I build on the synchronized arm-and-body motion that rewarded me with that halfway checkpoint, a full rotation of the shoulders is all I have to think about to engineer a solid, on-line backswing position. The key here is *completing* the shoulder turn and feeling this connection between the arms and upper body as you reach the top. As I use my right knee

as a brace, the simple reminder *turn* encourages the full rotation of my left shoulder under my chin in the process of coiling my torso over the resistance of the lower half. There is a real sense of *stretching* my upper body as I load into my right knee and thigh, my weight supported down the inside of my right leg. Under any sort of pressure, I always found that making a conscious effort to complete my shoulder turn added a precious half-beat to my tempo, and this split-

second can make all the difference to your timing as you then reverse the gears and shift into the downswing. When you make a natural turning movement of the upper body, you don't need to think about what's happening down below—turning your stomach and your shoulders over the stability of the hips and knees will reward you with a properly "sequenced" backswing.

THE TRANSITION
SLOW AND UNWIND

EVERY GREAT PLAYER starts his downswing with a subtle reflexive action in his lower body—usually the left foot or left knee. The dynamics of a powerful recoil work from the ground up. My own feeling is that my left shoulder dominated my first move down (although in reality it is *ankle-knee*-then-hip-shoulder), and when I'm moving correctly, that signals the recoil toward the target. Once you've wound up the backswing with a full shoulder turn (you should be able to see your left shoulder as it turns fully under your chin), the gracefulness of this transition adds to its quality. The left knee, left hip, and left shoulder pull away from their opposite numbers, and there's a wonderful feeling of the arms and hands falling into a natural and powerful delivery position—a sequence I often rehearse in slow motion. As the downswing begins to unfold, that separation of the left knee and shoulder pulling away from the right clears the way for your upper body to "fire" and rotate through the swing. For every golfer—me included—the danger lies in hurrying the transition, and hence the reminder: *slow and unwind.* Building acceleration is a gradual process, so give the sequence time to unfold naturally. When you do, your reward is one of the sweetest sensations in golf as the forearms, hands, and the club fall into this "slot" before they are accelerated through the impact area.

THROUGH THE BALL
WATCH IT!

THIS IS OLD advice, and it's still the best. As I approach and swing through impact, my key thought, *watch it*, focuses my attention 100 percent on a spot on the back of the ball—often on a single dimple. (That's my "No. 1 spot," fractionally inside the center line, if you can imagine that running through the ball—and exactly where I'm aiming to make contact.) Thanks to a smooth changing of gears through the transition, there's a wonderful sense of freedom as the body movement clears the way for my hands and forearms to release the clubhead *through the ball*. Note that I've maintained my spine angle all the way from the setup position (a *must* for consistency) while my legs continue to offer stability and balance to the rotation of the upper body as I unwind toward the target.

Of course, the moves you make through the downswing are both instinctive and reactive. But at the same time, the way you visualize the nature of impact generally can have a tremendous bearing on your development as a ball-striker. I played my best golf when I was "playing to a picture," seeing and feeling the desired flight of the ball, my hands and forearms very much alive to the shape of the shot that I had identified in my mind. This makes for an interesting discussion in Chapter 5, "Working the Ball," and one of the most valuable lessons I want you to take from this book is that impact is not a moment frozen in time but a passing-through area, an impact zone that extends a foot or so *before* the ball all the way to the finish. When you begin to think in those terms, you will take a big step forward in your ability to find a "slot," to put the clubhead on a rail all the way through the shot to a balanced finish.

THE FINISH
LOW HANDS

HAVING A CLEAR image of your swing's ultimate destination can significantly improve the quality of the moves that get you there. *Low hands* always inspired me to keep my arms swinging in close harmony with the rotation of my torso all the way to a wraparound finish, shoulders virtually level, chest and belt buckle facing *left* of the target. Pulled around by the momentum of the clubhead, my arms and hands swing over my left shoulder to a fully recoiled position, my weight supported securely on my left side as my knees work gently together. In fact, there's another good thought: *Kiss the knees.* I see a lot of amateurs who are reluctant to release their right leg, but doing so creates the most natural body lines in a poised and balanced finish.

Remember, your follow-through is a statement of intent, and knowing where you are headed before you start swinging will help you to release the clubhead freely and correctly through the impact zone. To experience the benefits a fully recoiled follow-through position promises, try making a few practice swings with this as your starting position. Rotate all the way through until your chest is facing left of target, hands low behind your neck, weight on the left side, right knee kinked in—hold that pose for several seconds and then fall into a graceful swing from there, looking for those same sensations as you return to that finish.

PRESSED FOR TIME?

FOCUS ON THE ABSOLUTE *MUSTS*

"**M**Y KEY Thoughts" really sets the agenda for the way in which we are now going to look at the details of the fundamentals (Chapter 2) before working through the process of "layering" a series of three easy backswing moves one on top of another to give you the initial links in a synchronized chain reaction. And the word I want you to keep in your mind as you prepare to go out and work on these lessons is *smooth*: How smooth can you make your backswing? Can you make the next one even smoother? One of my greatest assets was my tempo, and I want you to experience the benefits of a swing that embodies fluent motion. Tempo is the glue that holds a good swing together.

In the meantime, if you want to strip these swing thoughts to the bare essentials that can quickly

put you in touch with a good body motion, my advice is to focus purely on *Knees* at the setup to activate that sense of stability in your body core, *Turn* to complete your backswing, and *Through* to unwind all the way to a balanced finish. If you and I had just two minutes on the range, focusing on these three *musts* would form the cornerstones of a lesson that would give you the makings of a good athletic movement. There is nothing mechanical or complicated in these messages, but with that concept of a strong body action fixed in your mind's eye, I guarantee they have the power to significantly improve your basic swing shape.

■ ■ ■

LEFT *Knees*—sharpen your setup angles and engage core muscles with your weight on the balls of your feet.

CENTER *Turn*—maintain that athletic flex in your right knee and thigh as you rotate your belly and turn your left shoulder under your chin.

RIGHT *Through*—rotate your right shoulder all the way past your chin to achieve a balanced finish.

1987 *Open Championship Sunday, Muirfield*

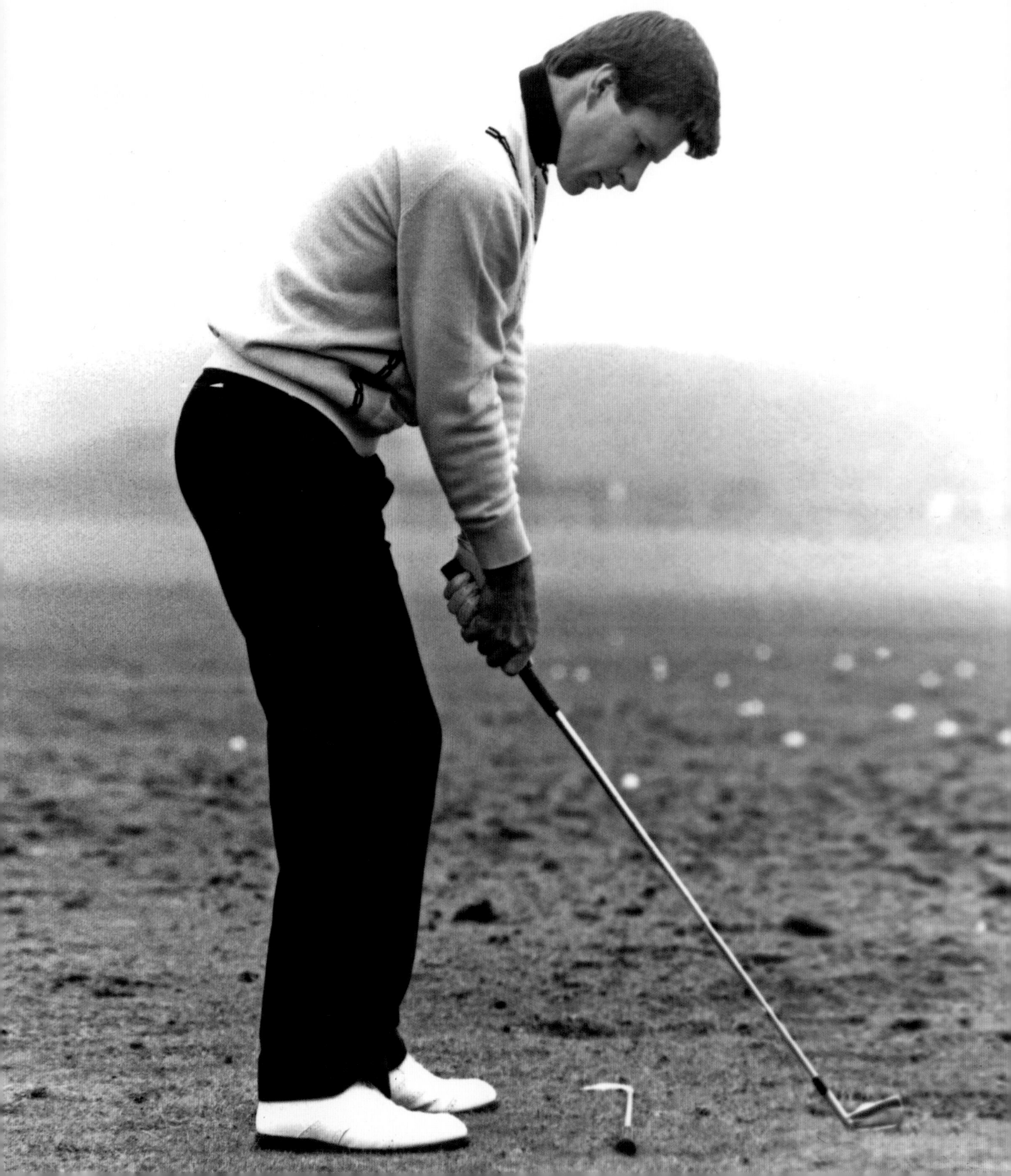

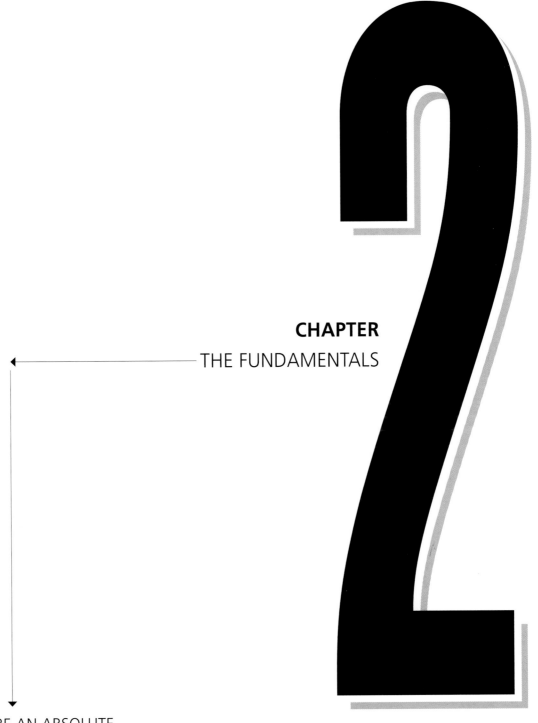

CHAPTER

THE FUNDAMENTALS

WHETHER YOU'RE AN ABSOLUTE BEGINNER OR THE BEST PLAYER IN THE WORLD, THE LESSONS YOU WILL ALWAYS COME BACK TO ARE THOSE THAT REVOLVE AROUND THE FUNDAMENTALS—**THE BARE ESSENTIALS FOR A SOLID, REPEATING GOLF SWING.**

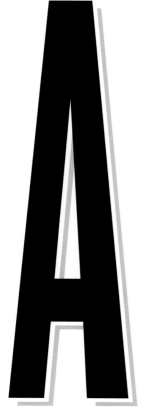

QUARTER of a century later, my memories of that life-changing week at Muirfield in 1987 are still vivid. I turned 30 on the Saturday of the Championship and celebrated with a level-par 71, solid golf in dank and misty conditions and, alongside opening rounds of 68 and 69, good enough to place me just a shot off the lead. I can remember sitting in my hotel room in North Berwick that evening and telling myself that my "apprenticeship" was finally over. I'd done my time. The swing that had taken the better part of two years to remodel and refine with coach David Leadbetter was running like a dream, and for the first time in my career I had the ball on a piece of string.

My confidence had been spurred by a notable ball-striking week at Gleneagles during the Scottish Open, the traditional curtain-raiser to the game's oldest championship. With my thoughts already on the specific "linksy" shots that I would need at Muirfield, I played all four rounds of that tournament in what I used to call my "Sam Snead mode"—making myself "club up" on approach shots, taking a 5-iron when the distance ordinarily suggested a 6, continually reminding myself to "swing easy."

A smooth tempo helps to soften the transition in the swing, giving you a lovely feeling of control as you unwind, and produces less spin and a lower ball flight—exactly what you need to "cheat" the seaside wind. I had also been experimenting with a simple "thumbs-up, thumbs-up" drill (described fully in the following chapter), harmonizing the movement of arms and body as I made half to three-quarter swings, my focus on nothing more complicated than pointing the thumbs up to the sky on the way back and again on the way through. Condensing the key moving parts of my swing had further reinforced my control of the clubhead—as long as I took care of the fundamentals, the swing would take care of itself.

The black-and-white prints you see here still give me goose

steps. But once I was on the range, 90 minutes or so before tee-off, it was business as usual. Photographer Peter Dazeley captured the mood succinctly in a handwritten note he made on the reverse of a print of the setup position: "*Nick Faldo, 4th round, Sunday July 19th—he practices with a club laid on the ground!*" Standard procedure for me—as it should be for you. As I prepared to depart for the most important round of my life, tried and trusted fundamentals took center stage.

Placing a club on the ground goes all the way back to my junior days at Welwyn Garden City. All through my swing build with David, I relied on that familiar source of reference to confirm my lines and levels were in order before I set to work on developing a swing that had its DNA set in the quality of that posture and alignment. After all I had been through, the way things unfolded over the course of that final round really couldn't have been scripted any better—with 17 pars on the card, I stood in the 18th fairway, a 5-iron in my hands and the dreams of becoming a major champion resting on one more good iron shot. I swear that as I settled over the ball, I could see the faint outline of that club on the ground telling me that my lines and my levels were perfect—"just go ahead and pull the trigger."

The rest, as they say, is history.

bumps when I look at them. I had a 3:10 p.m. starting time for the final round on Sunday and had to resist the temptation to get out onto the practice ground too early. If ever a day called for a disciplined routine, this was it. My daughter Natalie was just 10 months old at the time, and we spent much of the morning playing, a wonderful diversion; she was on the verge of taking her first

THE SETUP
CRITICAL LINES AND ANGLES

TO RECAP: We are now firmly in the business of building a *repeating* golf swing—a chain reaction in which a series of good moves can be seen to complement one another. In terms of your ability to hit a ball at a specified target, this makes the initial starting position *the* most important link in the chain. So let's look at the related elements of alignment and posture that lie at the heart of a sound, athletic setup.

The first thing I do on the range is place a club on the ground running *parallel* to my target line—for me that's the all-important frame of reference: a *must*. For a full shot with a full swing, I stand with the insides of my heels roughly the width of my shoulders and my weight on the balls of my feet as I check that my lines are "square"

with the shaft on the ground. This is all it takes to establish and maintain consistent body alignment. As you stand in that posture, you want your feet, knees, hips, and shoulders running parallel with that line. Standing side-on to your target can distort your perspective, so hold a second club across your body to check that you are standing "parallel left" of your target line. Hold that second club above the club on the ground and then draw it to your body, pressing it across your knees, hips, and shoulders to check that each of the key elements is in tune.

Once I'm satisfied that my

ONCE YOU are in good posture, with your weight on the balls of your feet, your arms will find their natural position if you allow them to hang freely.

alignment is true, I turn my attention to the body angles that characterize a good "ready" posture. And the secret here lies in getting your weight onto the balls of your feet so that you really do begin to appreciate the feeling of strong athletic balance. Remember what I said in the introduction about golf being no different from many other dynamic sports in the

way you have to use your body to generate speed? It all begins here with the way you prepare to interact with the ground. And the best way I know to achieve the balance and the athleticism I'm looking for is to get my weight on the balls of my feet and then raise my heels half an inch until I feel a "springy" tension in my knees and thighs. It's the same feeling you might

have if you were about to dive into a pool. Keeping those heels off the ground and adding a gentle bend at the hips creates the spine angle, and without my even thinking about it, my rear end pushes out a little to counterbalance.

You're going to get tired of hearing me go on and on about how important the knees are in supporting good posture and stabilizing the rotation of the trunk, but there's simply no escaping it. As I pull a club across my hips and lower my heels gently to the ground, my No. 1 setup thought, *knees*, reinforces the stable, "alive" posture I'm looking for. The muscles in my legs are now engaged to support and stabilize the upper body, and there's a strong and warming athletic tension in the

PARALLEL LINES: Make that club on the ground a constant companion when you practice, and you will reap the benefit of a correctly aligned body position.

THE MAKINGS OF ROTARY MOTION

thighs as they gear up to work as the suspension unit in the swing.

The beauty of identifying good posture in this fashion is that you don't have to worry about the arms and hands—they will find their own natural position as you bend from the hips and let them hang freely in front of your body. We'll discuss the details of the grip in just a moment, but look at how orthodox this all appears as the palms of the hands come together. Free of tension, the hands fall almost directly below the chin, and if I place the right hand in position just beneath the left, a good neutral grip is all but complete.

One of the questions I get asked a lot is, how far from the ball should you stand in a good setup? Well, that problem is easily solved when you take a club and add the finishing touches to this setup routine. With the butt-end of the grip just visible above my left hand, I adjust my spine angle to get the sole of the club flush on the ground—and there's the ball position.

Naturally, the spine angle you create will vary according to the club you're using. With a driver, the longest club in the bag, you're required to bend the least; as you work down through the set, the shorter-shafted clubs require a more noticeable spine angle in order to ground the club correctly behind the ball. You don't have to

think about this—the sequence I have illustrated will take care of that detail automatically.

Building your posture from the ground up clearly has a number of benefits—not least rewarding you with a real sense of mobility as you learn to identify and enjoy the sensation of being poised on the balls of your feet. You really want to feel that you take energy out of the ground and use it to empower your posture. When you experience that feeling of athletic tension on the tops of your thighs, you can be confident that you've engaged the muscles in your stomach and abdomen that are crucial to harnessing the power and rotary speed of your "core." Opera singers, karate experts, boxers—anyone who needs to access those core muscles as a significant power source needs to have their weight on the balls of their feet. Golfers fall into that category.

VIDEO LESSON: ALIGNMENT
Placing a club on the ground for alignment is an absolute *must*. Here Nick Faldo illustrates a practice technique that he has used and trusted throughout his career.

VIDEO LESSON:
BALANCE AND POSTURE Nick Faldo demonstrates a simple routine that will reward you with a balanced and athletic posture, the perfect position from which to make a sound golf swing.

IN THE FINAL ANALYSIS, a good posture leaves you prepared to rotate your upper body around a consistent spine angle and support that motion with a stable leg action. Standing square to your target line gives you access to it—and the better your rotation, the more easily your arms and hands swing *around* your body on a path that returns the clubface square to the target at impact. This basic pivot exercise will help you to recognize the sensation of turning your shoulders around the axis of the spine. With arms crossed, focus on rotating your stomach and right shoulder together and feel the stretch as you wind up to a full 90-degree turn. Keep that right knee flexed, and feel how your weight is absorbed into the right hip and thigh as you complete your backswing turn. With your weight on the balls of

your feet, feel the way the sequence of rotation works from the ground up. It's a gradual winding of the spring as your knees, hips, stomach, and shoulders turn progressively further relative to one another in the process of building torque. This body rotation lies at the heart of a repeating swing—the powerhouse dictating the rhythm and the tempo of every shot you hit.

One more important note here in terms of the consistency of your setup. Be wary of your "dominant" side. Like the majority of golfers, I'm right-handed, which can occasionally cause the right side of my body to climb a little too high—that is, the right hip and right shoulder get too prominent. As a simple fix, at address, drop or lower your right butt cheek. This will help to level up your belt line and angle your spine correctly, "softening" the right hip and right shoulder into the desired position. (Note: Left-hand-dominant players would lower their left butt cheek.) #

THOUGHTS ON STANCE AND BALL POSITION

WHAT'S THE IDEAL width of stance as you work through the clubs? I get asked that important question a lot. Clearly there's a balance to be struck here between *stability* and *mobility*. If you stand with your feet too far apart, you will inhibit your ability to rotate your hips correctly and "load" into your right knee and thigh; on the other hand, if your stance is too narrow, you weaken the foundations and run the risk of losing balance during the swing.

The ideal width of stance is that which allows you to rotate your body correctly and shift your weight back and forth in concert with a pure swinging motion. It will vary just a little according to the club you're using. Again, you want to avoid extremes.

With the driver, I set up with the insides of my feet spread to the full width of my shoulders and play the ball well forward in the stance, somewhere between left heel and left toe, depending on the shot in mind. The oversize design of the modern driver compels you to move the ball forward in order to strike it at the very lowest point in the swing arc—ideally just on the rise to achieve the optimum trajectory for distance (more on that in Chapter 6). I certainly feel that my weight favors the right side—not overly so, but enough to give me the feeling of being behind the ball. I turn my right foot out a few degrees, which helps the rotation of my right hip as I "load" into my thigh, the left foot being slightly more open to facilitate the full rotation of my body toward the target at the finish. Otherwise the setup posture contains all of the usual wholesome ingredients: knees flexed, weight on the balls of the feet, and a feeling of standing up tall and poised to make an athletic turn.

In the modern game, the driver is a special case. For the majority of full shots—including fairway

DRIVER

6-IRON

woods and hybrids—I set up with the insides of my heels no farther apart than the width of my hips. That's my benchmark. For the driver, the insides of my feet would be shoulder-width, sometimes more. I always maintain that a good test of your stance is to do a couple of squats as you vary the width while finding the balance on the balls of your feet—how far forward can you tip/lean and remain in balance? You want to find the width that feels the strongest. Moving down through the shorter irons, from 6-iron to wedge, I then work a sliding scale, drawing my right foot in a hair toward the left with every club down. My weight distribution would follow that scale, being

relatively even to the middle irons and then favoring the left side a little more with those more lofted approach shots (reflecting the desire to strike down on the ball and "trap" it for spin and control). For all regular trajectory shots, the ball position remains a constant, played from a point approximately two inches inside my left heel. Being marginally ahead of the "flat spot" in my swing enables me to "trap" the ball as the club approaches the bottom of the swing arc (i.e., in the final moments of descent), which gives me the ball-then-turf strike I want for spin and control.

These are merely guidelines to follow and experiment with. Moving the ball position up to two or three inches in either direction is a basic technique that will influ-

ence the strike and trajectory a regular swing gives you, and that's information worth knowing. In the short game, especially, there is tremendous scope for this sort of manipulation, and we will we talk about working the scale, playing the ball off the left toe for higher, softer shots, and moving it all the way back to the right toe for lower, punchier approach shots.

STABILITY VERSUS MOBILITY:
The ideal width of stance is that which enables you to rotate and shift your weight in tandem with a pure swinging motion, and will vary just slightly through the bag. Similarly, the ball position is adjusted to reflect the strike you're looking for.

9-IRON

THE GRIP

A GOOD SWING HINGES ON IT

A LOT HAS BEEN written in recent years about a modern swing featuring "quiet" hands. I don't agree with the implication of that and never have. The feeling that I experience in the hands and forearms has always played a huge part in terms of the feedback that I use to keep my swing ticking over, especially when it comes to the art of shaping shots and controlling the ball in the wind with spin and that split second of impact/reaction to the image of the perfect shot in your mind.

At the height of my career, I was often labeled a "positional" or "mechanical" player, which

I can understand because I did spend a lot of my practice time working on drills and checking specific positions. But what these observations always failed to take into account was that the quality of my body action to a large extent disguised the skill of my hands and forearms, the artistry at the heart of my technique. Yes, I was "mechanical," if you want to use that word, in the way I could churn out the same swing time after time. "Reliable" and "consistent" would be the words I would choose. I was *repetitive*. I had the ability to put the club into the right slots time and time again, along with the feel in the hands and forearms to manipulate the flight of the ball with whatever trajectory and spin were necessary. *Feel within a framework*—that's the phrase I keep coming back to, and the ability to play in that way demands a grip that is versatile in the extreme.

When I talk to the talented young players on the Faldo Series around the world, I go to great lengths to stress the role of the hands and forearms in making a sound golf swing. The grip holds the key. The hands have to be sensitive and "alive" to the weight and balance of the clubhead in order to *swing* it. They must be placed on the grip in a way that gives you a keen sense of the clubface position relative to the path. The coupling must be flexible enough for your wrists to hinge without restriction and create a pure *swinging* motion.

The muscles in your arms and wrists need to be supple and flexible enough to conduct great speed with a driver one minute, and deliver a delicate touch with a wedge the next. I played my best golf when my arms felt "heavy" and my shoulders "syrupy," a sensation that originated directly from the quality of my posture and the pressure I applied to the club with my hands and fingers. Again, it's a matter of balancing feel with control. The ideal grip pressure is one that enables you to forge a close working relationship with the clubhead; you have to be able to *feel* it, move it, waggle it, and—ultimately—control it.

FITTING THE LEFT HAND
PROMOTE THE "HINGE"

THE KEY TO making a good grip is to avoid extremes. You don't want either hand overpowering the other. The trend among young tour players in recent years has been toward a slightly stronger left-hand grip—turning the hand to the right on the club to reveal three knuckles (as the player views it looking down on his hands at the setup). That is certainly preferable to a weak left-hand grip. And so my advice at the outset is that you experiment with a slightly stronger left-hand position as you search for the style that best suits you.

(Before we look at the finer details, I ought to point out that it's worth experimenting with the *order* in which you place your hands on the grip, too. Strangely enough, I discovered that I had a tendency to set up with the clubface fractionally closed when I started with the left hand; plac-ing my right hand on the grip and aiming the clubface before fitting the left not only helped me to square the clubface but also rewarded me with a better right-hand position. Keep that in mind when you work on making your grip—alternating your lead hand is a simple exercise that will give you a different *feel*.)

One of the dangers when fitting the left hand is running the shaft too high in the palm, which effectively leaves you with a left hand that won't hinge properly. The hand gets too much underneath the shaft of the club, and its movement is restricted. To avoid that problem, take note of the way the hands naturally rotate in toward your body just standing with your arms hanging by your side—that gives you a good clue as to the way they should be applied to the grip. I would often let my left arm hang naturally at my side and simply drop the club into its curled finger, which achieves the desired effect of running the shaft diagonally through the joint of the forefinger to a point just below the root of the little finger. This simple routine guarantees the club sits more in the fingers of the left hand, which not only mobilizes the left wrist but encourages the slightly stronger left-hand grip we are looking for.

As the fingers curl around the grip, secure your left hand in position with the last three fingers, effectively trapping the club against the fleshy pad at the base of the thumb. I find that my little finger, in particular, curls firmly around the thicker part of the grip, bonding all three together.

Looking at the detail, note that the thumb should rest comfortably to the right of the center, and it should also be "short" on the grip. Pinch it into a snug fit, so there is no gap between the thumb and root of the left forefinger. This is a *must*. A short left thumb (as opposed to one extended long and loose down the grip) is more effective in creating leverage in the swing, and it also makes it easier to correctly fit the right hand.

Now raise the club in front of your body and check your grip position face-on. There should

be a slight cupping evident at the back of your left wrist and at least two-and-a-half knuckles visible on the back of your hand. The V that you see formed between your thumb and forefinger (thanks to that short, snug thumb) should point toward the middle of your right shoulder.

As I mentioned a moment ago, the trend on tour has been toward a slightly stronger left-hand position (the hand turned a tad more clockwise on the grip), and it's certainly worth experimenting with. Just keep your eye on the position of that V and make sure you stay within the parameters outlined here. The practical advantage is that this left-hand position promotes the early rotation of the left forearm at the start of the backswing and gives the left wrist a head start en route to hinging fully and correctly. So look for at least two-and-a-half knuckles to be visible on the back of the left hand (indeed, experiment with three). And keep that hinge oiled with a light, sensitive grip pressure.

LAY THE CLUB in the fingers of your left hand, and as you secure your hold, check that your left thumb rests comfortably to the right of center on top of the grip (as you look down on it), and that it is pinched "short," not extended. With the left hand fitted, check that the V formed between your thumb and forefinger points toward the middle of your right shoulder.

FITTING THE RIGHT HAND

PALM MIRRORS THE CLUBFACE

WHEN IT COMES to fitting the right hand, I want the palm to be perfectly square to the leading edge of the clubface, just as I expect it to be at impact. With fingers spread, the right hand covers and fits against the left like a piece in a jigsaw puzzle. The clubshaft fits in the channel created as the second and third fingers curl under the shaft—these are the key pressure points on the right hand—while the left thumb has a ready-made niche beneath the fleshy pad at the base of the right thumb. To enhance this snug feeling, I exert a little downward pressure from the lifeline of my right hand on top of the left thumb. That seals things nicely.

How you choose to join your hands together comes down to feel and preference. Just make sure that when you join your hands, one doesn't dominate the other. I favor the overlapping Vardon grip, in which the little finger on the right hand rides piggyback on the left, nestling in the ridge created between the first and second fingers. This remains the most popular grip out on tour, and I've always preferred it for the way it encourages the hands to work as a cohesive unit. As an alternative, entwining the little finger of the right hand with the forefinger of the left—the interlocking grip— is often preferred by players who have smaller hands and fingers. Jack Nicklaus used this grip his entire career, which is why Tiger Woods also uses it. It's purely up to personal preference. I've experimented with this variation but always found the Vardon grip just suited me better, especially when it came to the feeling I enjoyed releasing the clubhead through the impact zone.

Interestingly, using the Vardon grip, I have always felt that the chief pressure was in the last three fingers of the left hand and the trigger finger of the right; with the interlocking grip, I found the pressure was felt more in the middle of the grip under the left thumb. You have to go out and try these variations to determine which best suits you. Whichever style you choose, don't underestimate the importance of "triggering" that right forefinger into position, hooking it around the shaft until it lightly brushes the tip of the right thumb. This makes for a heightened sensitivity in your right hand, and as soon as you have that feeling in the fingers, don't be surprised if you experience an overwhelming urge to waggle the clubhead, just to get a feel for it. In fact, cultivate that habit. Waggle the clubhead back and forth, and you will appreciate the potential for delivering the speed and power this trigger unit gives you. Remember, your right hand mirrors the clubface. It's also your primary source of feel. As long as you maintain a relaxed but firm, workable grip pressure, you'll enjoy a silky sense of touch between your right forefinger and thumb.

Here's an interesting point I

VIDEO LESSON: THE GRIP
As your only point of contact with the golf club, the grip is one of the most important fundamentals in the game— as demonstrated here by Nick Faldo.

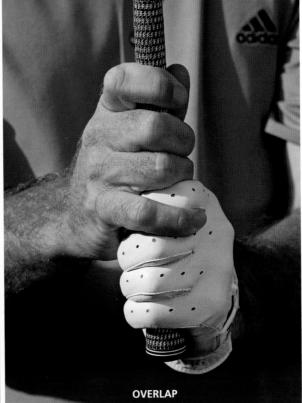

OVERLAP

INTERLOCK

BASEBALL

WITH YOUR fingers spread, the right hand fits like a jigsaw. As you complete your grip, hook the right forefinger around the shaft—"trigger" it into position. That immediately heightens your sense of "feel" for the club. Whether you prefer the Vardon, the interlock, or the baseball-style grip, make sure that the palm of your right hand is square with the leading edge of the clubface, and your grip pressure is such that the muscles in the wrists and forearms are relaxed.

discovered fairly recently: When you grip comfortably with the last three fingers of the left hand and the middle two of the right, tension is felt on the *underside* of the forearms; when you grip too strongly—particularly with the forefinger and thumb unit on either hand—that tension is felt on the *outside*, the topside, which you want to avoid at all costs. When the top of the forearms is relaxed, you can rotate and flow

the arms with the turning body; create tension there, and it runs all the way to the shoulders.

One particularly damaging fault I should mention is getting the right thumb too much on top of the grip, a super-strong hold more in keeping with grabbing a hammer. Players who make this mistake tend to be right-side

dominant not only at the setup but also at the start of the downswing. They experience an overwhelming urge to hit "at" the ball, forcing the right shoulder forward and "over the top." Be mindful of this. Any hint of tension is a killer. As soon as you tighten your hold on the club, you create muscular gridlock in your wrists, forearms, neck, and shoulders, which destroys any hope you have of making and repeating a fluent swing.

ROUTINE BUSINESS
VISUALIZE, PREPARE, RESPOND

ONE OF THE dangers of practicing on a wide-open range is that it's all too easy to lose your focus, and before you know it you've hit a bucket of balls without actually giving any thought at all to the quality of your alignment. With a glance at your target, you pull in one ball after another, and the problem is that after a while your body figures out a way of compensating for the fact that your shoulders are pointing 20 yards right or left. With repetition, you find some rhythm and hit the ball reasonably well and on line. Then you get out on the course and start thinking about what you're aiming at, and wonder why you're having trouble hitting a fairway or a green.

The only way to avoid this sort of scenario is to rehearse your pre-shot routine on the range and make alignment your first priority as you set up to the ball. In other words, get "target-oriented." Think about what you're trying to achieve. Don't stand there and drag in one ball after another—that defeats the object of rehearsing a routine. Take it one shot at a time. Stand behind the ball, study your target line, and get a clear visual image of the ball flying exactly the way you want it to. (Jack Nicklaus called this "going to the movies" on a shot—and made it his policy never to step in to the ball until he had that image crystal clear in his mind.) The golden rule, once you've done your homework, is that *everything revolves around the alignment of the clubface.* Your body takes its orders from there. Assuming a regular full shot, you simply aim

SEE THE SHOT   AIM THE FACE   SETTLE INTO POSTURE   WAGGLE

the leading edge squarely along the ball-to-target line and then adjust your stance and body position accordingly—feet, knees, hips, and shoulders—until you're square with that line. And with every single repetition of these good habits, they become more automatic on the course.

FOLLOWING a carefully rehearsed routine is certainly the best defense mechanism you can have under pressure; it gives you something positive to focus on and quiets the mind, no matter how much may be riding on a particular shot. The ultimate reward for all of that hard work on the range is the ability to switch to autopilot on the course, and good golf is then all about going through a series of well-rehearsed motions.

For me, a good pre-shot routine starts a long way before I reach the ball. I'm constantly in tune with changing conditions as I walk to the next tee or down the fairway between shots. My senses are alive to the elements, the potential trouble spots on a hole, and the general lay of the land. By the time I arrive at the ball, I have a pretty good idea of the sort of shot I want to play, the final countdown then revolving around identifying the exact yardage before hitting the "play" button and turning thoughts into action.

Once I've selected the club, I take one last look at the target from directly behind the ball before moving in. I lead with my right foot and aim the clubhead squarely down the target line before bringing in my left foot to take my stance and complete my alignment—my feet, knees, hips, and shoulders aimed parallel left of that target line.

Address the shot, not the ball—I don't remember where I first heard that advice, but it's right on the button.

Once I'm satisfied with my alignment, I finalize the details of posture from the ground up. I check the ball position in relation to my left heel, then flex my knees and go after that sensation of a springy tension in each thigh—the muscles in the legs

TAKEAWAY **TOP OF BACKSWING** **THROUGH THE BALL**

ADDRESS THE SHOT, NOT THE BALL: A well-rehearsed pre-shot routine will help you to combine a series of good habits in an automatic response to your target—and that's your best defense under pressure.

always keyed up to support the coiling of the torso. To enhance this feeling, I push out with the insides of the knees, and that braces my legs nicely. Finally, I keep my chin up so that my shoulders have room to turn, and I take a couple of gentle breaths to expand and then empty the chest and leave me relaxed. This ties in with some good advice Henry Cotton once gave me, which was to breathe out at the start of the backswing. Try it, and you'll find it helps you to get off to a smooth start.

I began to appreciate the importance of a waggle during my preparation at Gleneagles ahead of that momentous week at Muirfield in 1987. Those were the early days of learning to rotate my left forearm and "set" my wrists correctly at the start of the backswing, and rehearsing that sensation in miniature simply helped me to then find it for real in the swing. One of the great feelings that I always look for is that of the clubhead gathering speed early on as you move it away from the ball, and with a couple of waggles I found that I enhanced my feeling for the weight and balance of the clubhead, which encouraged me to *swing* it into the backswing. In fact, someone once referred to my swing as nothing more than a big waggle carried to the top with a good body turn. This is actually not a bad way to visualize it! Or,

REHEARSING the sensation of a good wrist-and-forearm action with the waggle helps me to find it for real in the backswing.

as my first coach, Ian Connelly, always used to say, "The swing is a giant pitch shot."

USED CORRECTLY, the waggle is a *mini*-swing, a sneak preview of what's to come. It's an opportunity to rehearse the wrist-and-forearm action that you intend to employ in conjunction with your body motion at the start of the swing. Hovering the club a few inches above the ball, I take a final look at the target while simultaneously rotating my left wrist and forearm in such a way that the club traces a natural inside path until it's virtually parallel with the target line. My right wrist hinges back on itself—exactly as I want it to in the swing now seconds from taking shape.

Remember, this is a preview of a series of subtle moves designed to combine *with* the rotation of the body to create a swing. It's not all about the hands and forearms,

and neither is it all about the body. The chain reaction of moves we're aiming for involves a blending of this wrist-and-forearm action with the heartbeat of the body turn—*feel within a framework* that promises a flowing, repeating golf swing.

No great player has ever moved from a static position at address. Every single one has a pressure release, a personal quirk or mannerism—shifting weight from side to side, a wiggle of the hips, anything that helps them to relax, engage with their key thoughts, and start their swing smoothly. Jack Nicklaus made use of a gentle waggle as he stared down his target, and then turned his head gently to the right to signal the start of his swing. Gary Player liked to trigger his swing with a pressing of the right knee. Five-time Open champion Tom Watson was always a great waggler of the club—a shake of the clubhead and then everything "fires." My co-analyst Johnny Miller was another good example of a player who used a brisk vertical waggle to prime his action. So experiment. You have to find your own trigger. Personally, I like to waggle the clubhead a couple of times to keep things moving and pep myself up for the swing I'm hoping to make. It's part and parcel of a setup position that exudes both motion and confidence in equal measure.

USED CORRECTLY, the waggle is a mini-swing, and a valuable opportunity to prime the wrist and forearm motion you're looking for in the initial moves away from the ball.

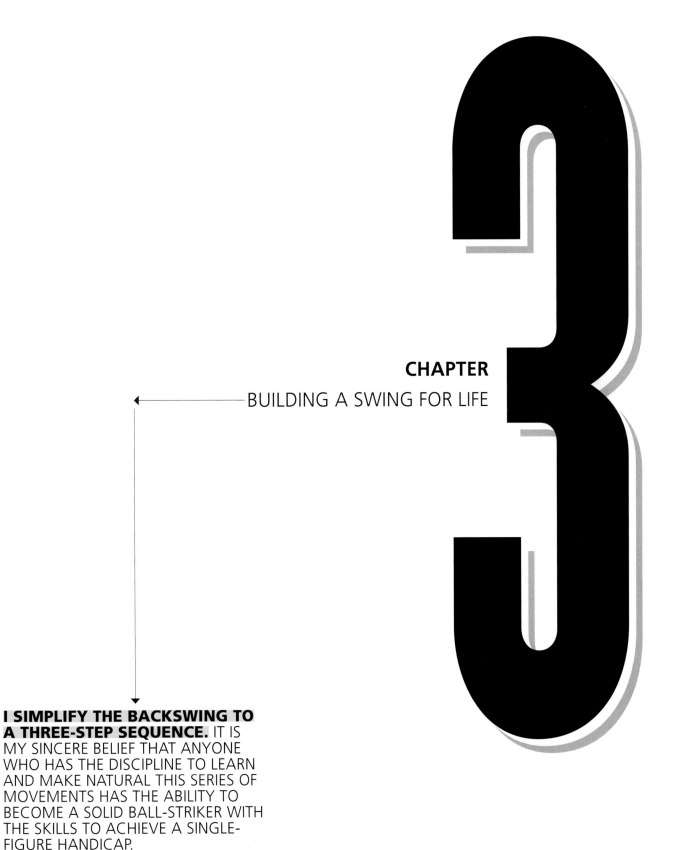

CHAPTER

BUILDING A SWING FOR LIFE

I SIMPLIFY THE BACKSWING TO A THREE-STEP SEQUENCE. IT IS MY SINCERE BELIEF THAT ANYONE WHO HAS THE DISCIPLINE TO LEARN AND MAKE NATURAL THIS SERIES OF MOVEMENTS HAS THE ABILITY TO BECOME A SOLID BALL-STRIKER WITH THE SKILLS TO ACHIEVE A SINGLE-FIGURE HANDICAP.

EFORE GOLF emerged on my radar, cycling was my passion. I enjoyed tinkering with my bikes almost as much as I did racing them, and my father always loves to tell the story of the time I had a new machine one birthday and spent a whole day taking it to pieces before putting it all back together and taking it for a spin. I guess that's just the way I'm wired. For me, the attention is always in the details. I like to know how things work. So it was really no surprise that when I made the decision to rebuild my golf swing in the mid-1980s, I soon found myself absorbed in the process of breaking it down into its various components before reassembling them in good working order. I didn't just want to understand my swing, I wanted to "own" it.

To my mind, breaking a problem into bite-size chunks that enable you to focus on the key elements of the bigger picture makes perfect sense. There are fortunate individuals out there who pick up a golf club and find making a swing as natural as walking, and yet the stats would suggest that most club golfers struggle to acquire a sound and *repeating* technique that enables them to enjoy a consistent level of ball-striking. This is where my experience of "layering" a series of good moves, one on top of another, serves as a logical formula to accelerate the learning process. The key, based on my own experience, is to focus on those moves you can realistically expect to control: the setup, the initial backswing sequence, and the follow-through position. The motion that takes place in between is *reactive*, and it happens at such speed that you cannot expect to exert much influence on it. (As I say in Chapter 1, "My Key Thoughts," familiarizing yourself with the nature of a good follow-through is an important and often overlooked aspect of the process—that familiarity with your final destination filters back through the chain, and can thus improve the moves that get you there.)

Over the years, as my own understanding has grown, I've simplified the backswing into a

three-step sequence of moves that you will find illustrated over the following pages. And as you practice them, I want you to always keep in mind the value of *rhythm*.

Remember, your goal is to blend these moves so finely that you end up with a pure, swinging motion—without that quality, a swing is just a series of good ideas. Ultimately, we are looking for a chain reaction, a movement that originates from a well-structured setup in a continuous motion based around the rotation of the body. Working on the individual links in that chain will help you understand where you're headed,

and also provide useful check-points along the way. But remember, these are *passing-through areas*, not destinations in their own right.

During the best ball-striking years of my career, I often found that my sense of motion came from the belly. I enjoyed a wonderful sensation of momentum with thoughts of turning and moving my forearms, my hands, and the club in tandem with my belt buckle, as if they were joined with an invisible piece of elastic. I mention this to illustrate how thoughts and feelings will just pop into your head as you work

on your swing and discover where your own sensory perception lies. When you practice, you will find that you isolate particular movements, or positions, and as you spend time fine-tuning them, certain thoughts will become extremely valuable to you. Write them down. Because when it comes to the business of putting all of the pieces together, your focus has to be 100 percent on the continuity and *flow* of your golf swing. That way, you will narrow the gap between your best and worst shots and establish a flight pattern that you can trust and control.

THE SETUP
GEARED FOR ACTION

NOW THAT YOU have in your mind that concept of a swing governed by the rotation of the body, you can understand the importance of fine-tuning the details of the setup. The club on the ground helps you align feet, knees, hips, and shoulders. That's a *must*. My No. 1 setup thought, *knees*, then adds that springy, athletic tension in the thighs that gears up the whole body in preparation to make a coordinated swing. As I bend from the hips, the arms hang freely, placing the hands directly beneath my chin.

I make no apologies for the fact that I continue to stress the importance of posture and the setup position. The angles you create with your body—and most importantly the spine angle—determine the axis about which you turn and the quality of your body motion generally. Maintaining good body angles as you wind and unwind your body to impact will give you the best possible chance of making solid and consistent contact—and to achieve that, you need this stabil-

ity in the body core. The bouncing drill (overleaf) is really useful to get the sensation of flexing the knees and thighs, and when you rehearse this, I want you to be aware of the muscles in your rear end and the vital part they play in establishing *core stability* in a good posture. The better your stability in this area, the better your chances of making and repeating a dynamic swing.

As soon as you compromise your body action, you create the need for compensation as the plane of the swing changes, which essentially means recovery with the hands and arms. And that is never reliable. This is why the young stars of today work predominantly on

IN GOOD POSTURE, the athleticism you enjoy in the knees and thighs will promote the core stability that is so vital in terms of maintaining good body angles during the swing.

core strength and flexibility in a bid to increase the efficiency of their rotary motion and develop more speed. For anyone serious about achieving their true potential in the game, golf-specific exercise designed to strengthen the core muscles—regular stretching, medicine ball training, and so on—is the way forward. A good body action is the chassis; the better you maintain it, the stronger and more reliable it will be.

DRILL

FEEL BALANCE ON THE BALLS OF THE FEET

MANY GOLFERS BELIEVE the setup to be a static position. That's not the way I see it. A good setup is dynamic and always promises a coordinated, athletic movement. Now is the time for your brain to be sending messages out to your body, reminding all the muscles of what you hope to achieve with the swing. I've said it before and I'll say it again: One of the best ways to achieve good posture and core stability is to think of the knees. Having assumed your position over the ball, lift your heels a half-inch or so and find your balance with your weight supported on the balls of your feet before settling your heels back on the ground. Use the muscles in your thighs and rear end to counterbalance your upper body as you bend from the hips to create that spine angle, and hold it right there for a couple of seconds. With your arms hanging comfortably and your chin nicely up off your chest, you have the makings of a great posture and setup position. To complete the exercise, gradually lower your heels back down, but keep that sense of being on your knees and thighs—the muscles in your legs must feel strong and lively, ready to support the coiling of the upper body.

Bear in mind, also, the point I made in the previous chapter about being wary of becoming right-side dominant (or left side for left-handers). Lowering the right butt cheek slightly at address will help you to "soften" the position of the right hip and right shoulder, and thus create the angle across the shoulders you are looking for.#

THE FIRST MOVE
MOMENTUM FROM THE WORD "GO"

THE KEY TO establishing momentum and a unity of purpose lies in working everything away *together*. By that, I mean the club, hands, arms, stomach, and shoulders are all involved in turning away from the ball in one synchronized movement. (Remember what I said a moment ago about that invisible strand of elastic between the belt buckle and the hands on the grip?) As my hands pass the outside of my right thigh, I look to see that the club is pointing to 8 o'clock on an imaginary clockface. That confirms my first checkpoint.

Rehearse this in slow motion: Everything turns away from the ball, and you feel your weight flow across to the right side; there's a gradual building of pressure down the inside of your right thigh and a resistance on the ball of your right foot. I've always liked the feeling of the upper part of my left arm maintaining contact with the upper left part of my chest as I do this—that always helped to keep me "connected." Meanwhile, the natural geometry of the swing sees the clubhead remain outside the hands as it traces a natural path inside the ball-to-target line.

You will relate to other thoughts and feelings personal to you as you repeat this move. Maintaining the relationship between your forearms as you turn your stomach and club together might do it; moving your belt buckle in time with your hands and the club to 8 o'clock might work better. I like to imagine my stomach invisibly attached to my hands and the grip, and the gentle rotation of my left forearm being integral to the initial movement away from the ball. I also like the sensation of my left shoulder working down and across.

All that really matters is that you establish this initial momentum with a sense of togetherness as your hands, forearms, and stomach combine to point the clubhead to 8 o'clock. Your spine angle provides the natural axis about which your shoulders are now beginning to turn, while your wrists and forearms reveal signs of that early rotation primed with the waggle. You're off and running.

WITH A COORDINATED MOTION, the club moves in tandem with your hands, arms, and belly to this key 8 o'clock checkpoint.

STOMACH, ARMS, AND CLUB "TOGETHER"

HERE'S THE MOST effective way I know to experience the bundle of sensations associated with this critical, all-encompassing first move away from the ball. For the ease with which it rewards me with the feelings of "rotation" and "togetherness" during the initial backswing sequence, this exercise has become one of my standards.

Why the split stance? There's a good reason for it. Placing your left toe inside the shaft on the ground and your right foot forward of it immediately creates a little resistance in your right hip and thigh—a resistance you then rotate *against* as you work on moving your stomach, arms, hands, and club "together" to that 8 o'clock position. Gripping down the shaft of a club until the butt-end rests in your belly button gives you a terrific feeling of the way in which the stomach and the unit of the arms, hands, and club are connected. The objective is simply to keep the butt-end of the club in contact with your stomach as you rehearse this initial sequence.

As you will quickly discover, the key to doing this successfully lies in rotating your stomach in unison with your arms and the clubhead. With your weight on the balls of your feet, feel the way in which you rotate against the flex in your right knee and thigh—"load" across and into your right side. With this exercise, not only do you consolidate good movement of your stomach, arms, hands, and club together, but you experience the initial sensations of coil as you turn your torso over the hips and knees.#

TO HALFWAY

GATHER SPEED AS YOU SWING UP "IN BALANCE"

N OW THAT YOU'VE forged that all-important first link in the chain, let's turn our attention to the forearm, hand, and wrist action that you need in order to swing the club up on the correct plane— or "in balance," as I prefer to think about it. As you move through the 8 o'clock position, the key now is to build on that momentum while you involve the wrists and forearms to translate turning into a *swinging* motion.

I've always loved the feeling of the clubhead swinging early, the gathering of pace as the club-head works up in the backswing. The way you string the opening moves together enables you to enjoy that feeling. I work through the 8 o'clock position so my left forearm and left wrist continue to rotate gently away from the target, while at the same time my right elbow "softens" and my right wrist hinges back on itself (all primed in a good waggle!). And though this may sound complicated, I think you'll find these moves gel quite easily if you rehearse them in slow motion. As your left arm continues to rotate across your chest, the full hinging of your wrists occurs somewhere between the

time your hands pass your right thigh and the moment your left arm reaches the horizontal. No hard-and-fast rules, but that's a good frame of reference.

Through the best years of my career, I'd say this was the single most important position I looked for in the everyday maintenance involved in keeping my swing "in the slot"—my hands, arms, and body in perfect timing. This is your reward for all that hard work fine-tuning the details of your grip, alignment, and posture angles. Together, these fundamentals enable you to set in motion a sequence that leads you through 8 o'clock to the security of this halfway-back "set" position. Checkpoints don't come much better than this: My arms, hands, and body are working in unison; the club is on line and in balance; the rotation of the body is poised to complete the coil. As long as I maintain that flex and resistance in my right knee and thigh, and the stability in the core area in general, everything is plugged in for a solid position at the top.

DRILL

MEET YOUR HALFWAY-BACK CHECKPOINT...

A SERIES OF THREE related drills will help you to identify with the sensations you're aiming for as you swing *through* the 8 o'clock position to this key halfway checkpoint. First, a simple exercise: From the setup position, all I want you to do is make as if to shake hands with someone standing directly to your right—turn and move your outstretched right hand to that "How do you do?" position. In so doing, you will automatically rotate your upper body while your right wrist gently hinges back on itself. You want the palm of your hand to be parallel with the target line, and it should appear to be directly in line with the middle of your chest.

The one thing you have to be wary of here is a reluctance to move off the left side; if you don't "let go" and turn your hips, or are simply inclined to keep your weight rooted on the left side, the palm of your right hand will most likely point down to the ground, and you will be forced into "cheating" the correct handshake, and do it all with your arm and hand only! So as you rehearse this exercise, make that commitment to turn and shake—"How do you do?"

To complete the drill, grip a club in your left hand and swing it around to join the right—and bingo! You are now on line and on plane approaching the critical halfway stage in the backswing. Look for the same sensations when you then move through these positions in the swing for real. As illustrated further overleaf, the split-stance is key to the dynamic of this exercise for the way in which it reinforces that all-important resistance in the right knee and stability in the core area as you work through these early positions to reach the set halfway checkpoint—soak up the sensations as you hold this position. You should be aware of a slight increase in tension into your right thigh and a stretching of the muscles in your stomach as you prepare to embark on the process of fully turning and "loading" into that right side.#

ROTATE AND SET AGAINST A BRACED RIGHT KNEE AND THIGH

I'VE ALWAYS WORKED on the principle that my wrists should be fully "set" by the time my left arm reaches the horizontal in the backswing, and to get there I made a conscious effort to rotate my left forearm in a clockwise direction and really crank the wrists as I move the club through the 8 o'clock position and wind my upper body over the resistance of my knees. The handshake drill gives you the sensation of the position you want to work *through* as you synchronize your arm and body movement to achieve this full "set."

The split-feet position again makes for a terrific exercise as you focus on layering these backswing moves one on top of another, continually fine-tuning the wrist-and-forearm action so vital to swinging the club up "in balance." Placing your right foot ahead of your left simply intensifies the athletic sensation of turning and winding your upper half over the resistance of your right knee and thigh, shifting and containing your weight with the quality of that lower body action. (You will also discover what lack of mobility you have

in your lower body—unless you get to the gym, there could be 20 yards of distance logjammed in there!) Repeat this from the setup. Focus on maintaining that flex in the knee as you work through the earlier sensations (8 o'clock to the handshake move), and enjoy the feeling of "setting" the wrists and swinging the club up in perfect balance.

With these relatively simple drills, you are now more than halfway to a solid backswing position—the chain reaction is well under way. The more you rehearse these drills, the sooner they will gel together. And keep in mind your grip pressure and the need to remain fluid and supple. Any sign of tension will kill the motion in its tracks. Run through the sequence at home in front of a mirror; spend a few minutes on the range before you hit balls to cement positive feelings as you blend the movement of your arms and the club with the rotation of your body. Once the club is on plane, or in balance, all you have to do is complete your shoulder turn for a full backswing coil.#

VIDEO LESSON: THE TAKEAWAY
As the first link in the chain, the takeaway is vital in setting the tone of your golf swing. Here, Nick Faldo demonstrates a drill that will help you to coordinate your motion, encouraging the hands, arms, stomach, and club to work together.

DRILL

LET THE CLUB FIND ITS "BALANCE POINT"

A **LOT OF GOLFERS** get themselves tied up in knots over the concept of swing plane. I've learned over the years to simplify what's needed. I played my best golf thinking of nothing more complicated than swinging the club up in good "balance." To get this feeling, take a club lightly in a "pencil" grip between the thumb and forefinger of your right hand and spend a few minutes swinging it freely back and forth. To add some momentum, start the club a few feet ahead of the ball and let it fall and gather pace as you swing it up to halfway. With no manipulation, it will find its natural balance point, and it will feel light in the hand as you hold it there. The plane of your swing will naturally vary a little between clubs, but as a general rule, I look for the shaft to cut through the tip of my right shoulder. That's a fairly standard point of reference. And that's as complicated as it needs to get.#

TO THE TOP
"COMPLETE" WITH A FULL TURN

COMPLETE: Turning the left shoulder fully under the chin is one of the simplest and most effective swing thoughts—one that will reward you with a fully coiled backswing position.

. . . AND HERE'S the reward. From the safety of that halfway "set" checkpoint, I've simply turned my shoulders through a complete 90 degrees to achieve this fully wound-up backswing position. There's a terrific feeling of rotating and stretching the bigger muscles in my torso as my lower body continues to offer that resistance—a strong sense of turning against that braced right knee. I'm also aware of an increasing tension down the inside of my right thigh as the majority of my weight is now supported on my right leg.

The rear view of the swing is most telling. When you look in the mirror, it ought to be clear that your shoulders have turned about

VIDEO LESSON: TURN
Completing your shoulder turn is one of the keys to consistent timing—and also a great pressure release, as Nick Faldo explains.

the natural axis of your spine— one of my absolute *musts*—while your hands and arms have simply followed the lead of your body rotation. One specific point here: Note that my right elbow is allowed the freedom to work away from the body—that's important. I see many amateurs who keep that elbow glued to their side, which denies them any hope of creating width in the backswing. Don't be afraid of letting the right elbow find its own space; as it does so, you will enjoy greater freedom through the transition in readiness to get the club into the slot approaching impact.

Turn—that really is the key here. We all have a tendency to become "body-lazy" if we haven't played for a while, and so reminding yourself to *complete* your backswing turn is one of the most effective thoughts you can have. In so doing, you add that vital half-beat to your swing that takes the club to a full position at the top with a proper coiling of the upper body. For that same reason

it's also one of the great pressure releases—any time you feel yourself becoming tight, just think about getting that left shoulder fully under your chin. The pure dynamics of a sequenced and fully coiled backswing position will then lead you almost involuntarily into the downswing, as you get set to throw the gears into reverse and gather momentum into the downswing.

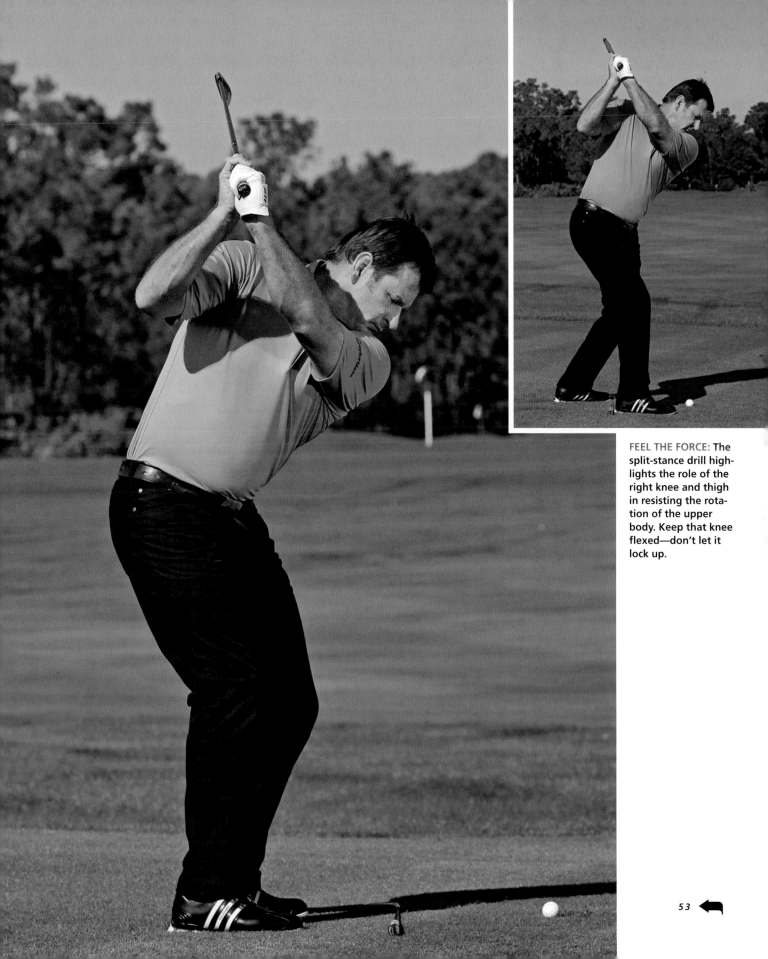

FEEL THE FORCE: The split-stance drill highlights the role of the right knee and thigh in resisting the rotation of the upper body. Keep that knee flexed—don't let it lock up.

DRILL

PRESET + TURN FOR A SOLID BACKSWING

WHAT DOES A good backswing feel like? Combining a good wrist hinge with a full body turn, this "preset + turn" drill will quickly put you in touch with the sensations you're looking for in a "loaded" position at the top. It works like this: Starting in a good setup position, hover the club above the ball and then (keeping the elbows level) hinge your wrists to set the shaft up as close to this 45-degree angle as you can get it. Hold that position for a couple of seconds and then turn your left shoulder under

your chin to wind your upper body and swing the club to the top of the backswing. That's a solid backswing in two easy moves. Check that you've maintained your spine angle and that your right knee has absorbed the transfer of weight into the right side. As you become comfortable with this routine, try hitting a few balls. Set the wrists, turn the shoulders—bang! When you get to the top, you'll be certain you're in the right position. Tee up the ball to do this—the quality of the motion is more important than the quality of the strike, so make it easy on yourself! Set the wrists, turn your body, and release. That's a great confidence booster.#

DRILL

THE ANTI-ROLL MECHANISM

WE OFTEN TALK about keeping the clubhead outside the hands during the first few feet of the takeaway, and this little drill can help you to experience that feeling. It's especially good for those of you who tend to roll the hands, forearms, and clubface away from the ball on a severely inside path. To counter that, take your setup position and then work your hands inside as you move the club away from the ball so that the butt of the grip brushes your right thigh. As you do so, be aware of your weight just "bumping" across onto the ball of your right foot, and hold it there a second—that's your checkpoint move. Then go ahead and crank the wrists as you turn your shoulders to swing the club into the backswing. If you're susceptible to rolling the club at the start of the backswing, you're also likely to inhibit the width of your swing as your right elbow is tucked in to your right side. So give yourself a little more freedom; let it float behind your body into a full, wide position at the top. Hit balls doing this—tee them up and enjoy a sensation of width you won't have experienced in a while.#

EXPERIENCE WIDTH WITH RIGHT HAND ONLY

LOTS OF GOLFERS deny themselves the pleasure of making a full and wide backswing because they insist on keeping their right elbow tucked in to the side of their body. Doing that narrows the backswing arc and damages the relationship between the unit of the arms and upper body. Here's a simple way to overcome that tendency: Make a series of rehearsal swings with just your right hand on the club, going down the shaft so that it assumes its regular position on the grip. Flex your knees as you prepare your setup, grip lightly so you can feel the weight of the clubhead on the end of the shaft, and then go after the sensation of *swinging* it all the way to a full and wide backswing position. You have just one hand on the grip, so there's no danger that you'll over-control the club, and as a result you'll enjoy better "sequencing" of the arm and body motion.#

THE TRANSITION

UNWIND FROM THE GROUND UP

GOOD FOOTWORK is the mark of an accomplished player, and nowhere is the quality of the interaction you have with the ground more valuable than in the transition. As you reach the top of your backswing, you are at the same time starting down, creating a harmonic effect. For a split second your body is actually working in two directions at once: Just as the arms and the club complete their journey to the top, the left side of your body (in a sequence that runs knee-hip-shoulder) re-rotates toward the target, the resulting "lag" in the swing adding a silky quality to the acceleration you enjoy on the way down.

The one thing you don't see in a good transitional move into the downswing is aggression. This is a moment of softness, the calm before the storm. Jack Nicklaus used to call it a "gravity move," an expression that paints a wonderful image of the hands and arms falling momentarily as the left knee reverses the momentum back toward the target. As your weight flows back across to the left side, the right "holds" for a split second, long enough for the body to settle in readiness for the burst of speed as the recoil takes over and you have the green light to unwind hard through the ball.

Precisely what triggers your downswing will be personal to you—and it will vary from one day

to the next as your feel is drawn to the next area of the body. I always liked to think about pulling the left shoulder away from the chin to create a "separation." The green light that enabled me to do this was a natural unwinding from the ground up, allowing me to hold on to the angle in the wrists. Reversing the momentum is reversing the sequence. The full rotation of the shoulders added the final tightening of the coil, and now, to release the pressure, the process is reversed: The left knee, hip, and then shoulder re-rotate to the target, and in that split second the delay, or separation, rewards me with the opportunity then to unwind the whole of the right side through the impact area and all the way to a finish.

I**T ALL BOILS** down to that magical ingredient: *timing*. The great danger here lies in hurrying the change of direction from backswing to downswing and being too aggressive too early (typically) with the right arm and shoulder, a fault that results in throwing the club forward and onto a steep angle back to the ball. If you took a straw poll of the longest hitters in the game, and asked each of them to nominate a thought for distance, I guarantee that most would say they try to start the swing *easier*. They give themselves time to fully unwind. Which is why my key thought here is just that: *slow and unwind*. Another great feeling is staying on that right knee and thigh for a split second as you separate from the top, hanging on to the angle in the wrists. (You could also try *smooth and unwind* as a cue to your downswing; "smooth" is probably a better command than "slow," as it applies to all tempos.) There's no worse feeling in golf than driving off the right side too early, getting narrow and trapped as you approach the ball. Wait for it a moment, give your body dynamic the time it needs to reverse the sequence, and unwind from the ground up. That way, you can look forward to releasing the club with perfect timing through that extended impact zone, arms and hands totally in sync with the re-rotation of the body core.

WHAT "FIRES" YOUR DOWNSWING?

CAN YOU "SETTLE" in the transition while keeping your rear end in position? That's a good way of rehearsing the downswing, as holding that position for a split second gives the upper body time to shallow the plane and fall into a good hitting position. The move you see me making here is an exaggeration, clearly, but it gives you some idea of the "squat" position we're looking for as a result of a good transition at the top. Rehearse this in slow motion, and then make this a natural separation when you run it at normal speed.

It's important to experiment initiating the downswing sequence using different triggers. Here I'm leading the way with the left knee, creating the "squat" and separation that will benefit the recoil. Much of the time my focus would be on pulling the left shoulder away from the chin; that was always a favorite, creating a feeling of separation before unwinding through the ball. If I wanted to

protect against the ball going left, I would focus on rotating the left side of my body a little harder so that it was always ahead of my hands; to play a right-to-left shot, I would think about quieting my body action and encourage the left shoulder to move up slightly through the transition while allowing the rotating forearms to be more in-volved.

You can, and *should*, fine-tune that dynamic to suit your own preferences.

There are no limits to this exploration. What happens if you place your emphasis on the left knee, using that to trigger your downswing? Al-ternatively, how does focusing on the re-rotation of the left hip affect ball flight? When your body is working really well, you can place all your emphasis on what your arms, elbows, and hands are doing. When I'm looking for distance, I think about a fast belly and *fast elbows*—there's another great feeling. Any time I had the luxury of focusing on what my elbows were doing, I could be darn sure that my body was wind-ing and unwinding in perfect sequence. Having wound up a good backswing, you have all this to discover as you learn to unwind the spring with more and more confidence. You need to find the trigger that enables you to unwind in sync.#

VIDEO LESSON: THE TRANSITION
Nick Faldo highlights the sensations involved in mastering the change of direction at the top of the swing—a subtle series of moves that rewards you with the green light to unwind through the ball.

FIND THE INSIDE PATH TO IMPACT

G OLFERS WHO TEND to grab the club with a "strong" right-hand grip (typically too much in the palm and with the thumb either on top of the shaft or even slightly right of center) invariably make a swing that is right-side domi-

nant. And that inevitably leads to hitting "at" the ball from the top. The urge to use the right shoulder hijacks the transition, and the classic "over-the-top" move throws the club onto a severe out-to-in path. Result? A steep downswing, cutting across the ball, massive loss of distance. If you recognize these symptoms, here's a drill that will help you "quiet" the transition and find the natural inside path to impact. Take a mid-iron and make a regular grip with just your right hand on the club. Go down the grip to where the right hand would ordinarily be placed and force your right thumb over into the correct position. (It will feel weak and uncomfortable, but I want you to persevere with it.) Then get into a good setup

position, allowing your left arm to hang freely, the palm of your hand open. The objective is to swing the club all the way back and then unwind to collect the open palm of the left hand. Start slowly, and gradually build your speed. Think about the transition. Let your right elbow swing freely behind your body and then feel the arm and the club shallow as you unwind from the ground up. Pretty soon you will replace that over-the-top move with a natural delivery from the inside, and collecting the left hand will become automatic. Repeat this a dozen times or more, and then hit a shot for real. *Speed squarely applied*—that's the secret to the most efficient transfer of the power you generate in your golf swing.#

COIL AND RECOIL— JUST LIKE THROWING A BALL

B**ELIEVE IT OR** not, I nailed the towel on the first take, but I've had a lot of practice. This is one of my favorite exercises to help golfers appreciate just how natural the coil-and-release movement we're looking for can be. Aiming to throw a ball hard at a target just a few yards ahead of where you're standing will warm up a good body

action and teach you to synchronize the flowing arm-and-hand action that accelerates the ball. *Coil* and *release*—just like a golf swing. The action is exactly the same as that of skimming stones across a lake; harmonized with the body action, the right arm shallows while the "lag" in the wrist is maintained deep into the throw before the hand adds the final burst of speed in releasing the ball. As you wind and unwind, you're shifting and containing your weight with an athletic body action. So, at the start of a practice session, position a towel as a target and loosen up by throwing a few balls at it as hard as you can. Where is your focus? ON YOUR TARGET! Not on what your

arm is doing—the arms and hand respond to your vision. You're not thinking, "Where is my right elbow?" or "Is it rotating at the right angle?" You are simply coiling and releasing in response to your vision and that target on the ground. Repeat the action over and over again. Having made a good backswing, loaded with energy, you are in a position to unwind and release your speed. With each throw, you're looking to create an instinctive reactionary move to a target—which is exactly what we're looking to achieve in a golf swing.#

THE PLAY ZONE
EXTEND YOUR IMAGINATION THROUGH IMPACT

IN CHAPTER 1, I introduced the notion of an extended impact zone, a professional way of thinking about the impact area as starting a foot or so before the ball and extending all the way through to the finish. Players who are able to grasp this more sophisticated notion of "impact" have a huge advantage when it comes to consistent ball-striking and the ability to "work" the ball at will. We'll discuss this in more detail in Chapter 5, where you'll also find a wonderful photograph of Ben Hogan approaching impact—an image that had a profound effect on my thinking back in the mid-1980s. Just moments from striking the ball, Hogan's delivery position appears so controlled and peaceful that it occurred to me he could do anything he liked with the clubhead. That photograph was pure inspiration to me as I rebuilt my swing in search of the tech-

nique that would give me similar control over my swing where it matters most.

More than anything, then, impact is a visual that you play to. I want you to replace thoughts of hitting "at" the ball with images of simply letting it get in the way of a flowing swinging motion as you unwind to a full and balanced finish. Think in terms of *collecting* the ball as you rotate your body and release the clubhead through the ball according to the image of the desired shot you have in

your mind. For me, thanks to that image of Hogan, the swing is not finished at impact; in fact, in many ways, it has only just started.

Of course, the quality of the positions that you swing through en route to the ball are largely determined by what's gone on before. That chain reaction is based on the reliability of a good body action and the rhythm with which you synchronize the motion of the arms, hands, and club. The better your transition into the downswing, the more freedom you'll enjoy through the hitting area—and the more you'll be able to *play golf* with the forearms and the hands. So as you work on your swing, recalibrate the way you think about impact. Don't be fixated on the ball: You are a better golfer the moment you think in terms of finding that slot and extending your impact area—the "play zone"—all the way through to a fully balanced finish.

IMPACT IS NOT a moment frozen in time as the clubhead meets the ball—it is an extended passing-through area starting a foot or so *before* the ball all the way through to the finish.

SWING HALF-TO-FULL

HERE'S A WONDERFUL drill that will help you think of impact as this extended zone just before the ball all the way to the finish. I call it swinging "half-to-full"—and the clue is in the title. Take a short iron and hit shots with no more than half a backswing, placing the emphasis firmly on the quality of your acceleration all the way to a full finish. Have some fun with this. Turn and hinge your wrists to reach that halfway checkpoint and then unwind and rotate all the way through the shot. That really does give you a great sensation of an extended play zone as you get the clubhead into that "slot" and whip it through the ball. When I work on this, I'm aware of rotating and swinging to the left of the target as I release the club through the ball—a natural opening of the body that clears the way for the arms to swing around to this finish. More than anything, this drill underlines the importance of the through-swing in the overall scheme of hitting solid golf shots. Which would you rather have, a full backswing and half a follow-through or half a backswing and a full release as you unwind to the target? No contest there. The more shots you hit using this drill, the less you will think about impact as being your destination. The quality of your ball-striking will improve no end as you extend that focus all the way to the finish—the entire release of the club through the ball matching the picture of the shot in your mind.#

DRILL

E PRESS TO PLAY . . .

VERYTHING THAT HAPPENS in the downswing has its origins in the backswing. The better you wind your body up, the more successfully you will unwind it down. That's why I work so hard on setting the club in balance and turning my body correctly. A good downswing is then a reflexive action and that extended impact zone the ultimate *passing-through* area. That said, gaining an appreciation of what a good impact position feels like makes for a valuable drill—one that I used regularly through my career. From a good setup position, the key is to morph into impact, and to do that you need to press the leading edge of the clubface into the turf to experience resistance. You want to feel that you exert pressure down through the forearms, the hands, and the chest working in harness as you simultaneously rotate the hips to the left of the target—hold that dynamic pose for several seconds. Your right knee will work on a line toward the left (it does not shoot out toward the ball), and your left leg is braced to absorb the strike. Soak in these sensations—they are valuable.#

THE FINISH
WRAP IT UP IN STYLE

BODY LANGUAGE PLAYS a vital role in learning to play good golf. Knowing where you want to finish your swing can actually improve the quality of the preceding links in the chain that get you there. That's why I'm a big believer in the benefit of rehearsing a good follow-through, holding the pose for several seconds to let the feelings really sink in . . . and then immediately looking to re-create them with a regular swing.

Bearing in mind the concept of extending the impact zone all the

THE COMPLETE rotation of the shoulders and chest to the finish governs the shape of a good follow-through— the logical conclusion to a fully committed golf swing, all wrapped up in perfect balance.

way to the finish, I'd say perhaps the word that best sums up this final position for me is *commitment*. On every full swing I make, there is a consensus of motion all the way through the ball to this balanced conclusion. At the heart of it all is that rotation of the body—the backbeat to a repeating swing. As a result of winding and unwinding the bigger muscles in my torso over the resistance of my hips and knees, the momentum of the clubhead has pulled the hands and arms into this wraparound finish—the total recoil. Note that my right shoulder points toward the target—that's a swing thought in itself—while the shaft of the club comes to rest against the collar of my shirt. There's still a little resistance in my hips and knees to support the position in balance, but basically I'm relaxed. Energy spent. Thanks to a supportive leg action, I could hold this position solid for several seconds.

The young stars on tour today

generate phenomenal speed with the rotation of their hips and body "core," and this is certainly an area to focus on in your effort to improve your recoil action. Having "settled" in the transition, think in terms of rotating your left trouser pocket and belt buckle as fast as you can in a counterclockwise direction left of target, clearing the way for your right hip, right shoulder, and chest to apply pressure on the ball through impact. In a logical chain of events, your right leg will then want to "release," the right knee working gently toward the left, which improves your posture lines at the finish.

Having the right knee gently "kiss" the left is one of the finishing touches I always liked—a sign of a job well done. In the final analysis, the majority of your weight is now supported on your left leg, while your right foot is balanced on its toe.

ROTATE AND UNWIND AGAINST A FIRM LEFT SIDE

I **N THE SAME WAY** that the right knee and thigh serve as the "post" against which you rotate and "load" a powerful backswing coil, the left side must present a certain amount of resistance to the rotation of your body in the through-swing. When we talk about the dynamics of impact, we often use the expression "hitting into a firm left side," and this exercise puts you in touch with what that actually feels like. The split stance this time sees the left foot placed ahead of the right, and the key is to brace that left knee and thigh as you prepare to swing and release the club against that resistance. When I do this, I experience a sensation of applying pressure down into the ball with the concerted efforts of my body core and forearms as I unwind against the resistance of the left knee and thigh. That's a great feeling to have, and it's one that translates into solid ball-striking.#

Favorite exercises to blend arm and body movement. You will find a number of useful swing exercises on the digital downloads—and here are two more favorites that will help you to synchronize hands, arms, and body for a sound, *repeating* golf swing. . . .

GIVE YOUR SWING THE THUMBS-UP!

AND SO TO the "thumbs-up, thumbs-up" drill I mentioned briefly in Chapter 2—a warm-up exercise that consolidates all the key moving parts in a solid golf swing. Combining wrist-and-arm action with the rotation of your body, it's essentially a means of turning the spotlight on the rotation of the arms and the correct hinging of the wrists as you make half to three-quarter swings, back and through. Using a 9-iron, I'm thinking only about warming up my body action as I rotate and coil my upper half over my hips and knees, hinging my wrists freely to point my thumbs up at the sky on the way back and again with a re-hinge on the way through. Start smoothly, and gradually build up your speed. Keep your knees solid. This really will reinforce what we are trying to achieve in terms of blending your arm swing and body rotation over a stable, resisting base. As you unwind, turn your body out of the way, get your hips "around the corner," and enjoy the feeling of a properly "connected" golf swing.#

SIMPLIFY THE FEELING OF ROTATION AND RESISTANCE

DURING THE SHOOTING of the photographs you see here, I was reminded of just how effectively this exercise enables you to experience what rotation and resistance in the arms actually feels like. The powerful coiling effect is possible only when a certain degree of resistance is present in your swing. And this push-palm exercise is one of the best to help you feel the sensation in your whole body as you wind and unwind.

It works like this: Take a club in your left hand and assume your regular address position, but cross your left wrist over your right, so that the back of your right hand rests against the back of your left. Now work on your swing in a smooth, continuous motion. As you make your backswing, you should sense that your right hand is pushing the left. Keep the flex in your right knee to resist the rotation of your torso, and feel the muscles in

the upper part of your back stretching like strands of elastic as you reach the top. Hold that position momentarily—feel that *stretch* in your upper body—and then unwind. In the downswing the left hand does the pushing, and this time you turn against the resistance of the left knee. At the moment of impact, it should feel like the back of your left hand is facing the target, and from there the rotation of the right side takes you all the way through to a full finish.

Not only will this exercise acquaint you with real sensations of stretch and resistance in the swing, but it also teaches you the correct rotation of both the left and right forearm. As long as you

keep the backs of your hands together, you will find that your arms rotate and fold correctly. Work on this drill in between hitting shots in practice, and also on the course whenever you need to remind yourself of good dynamics in motion.#

VIDEO LESSON: THE FOLLOW-THROUGH
Focusing on where you want to finish your swing can actually help you to improve the positions that get you there—and when you wrap it up in style, there's every chance you will hit a solid shot, explains Nick Faldo.

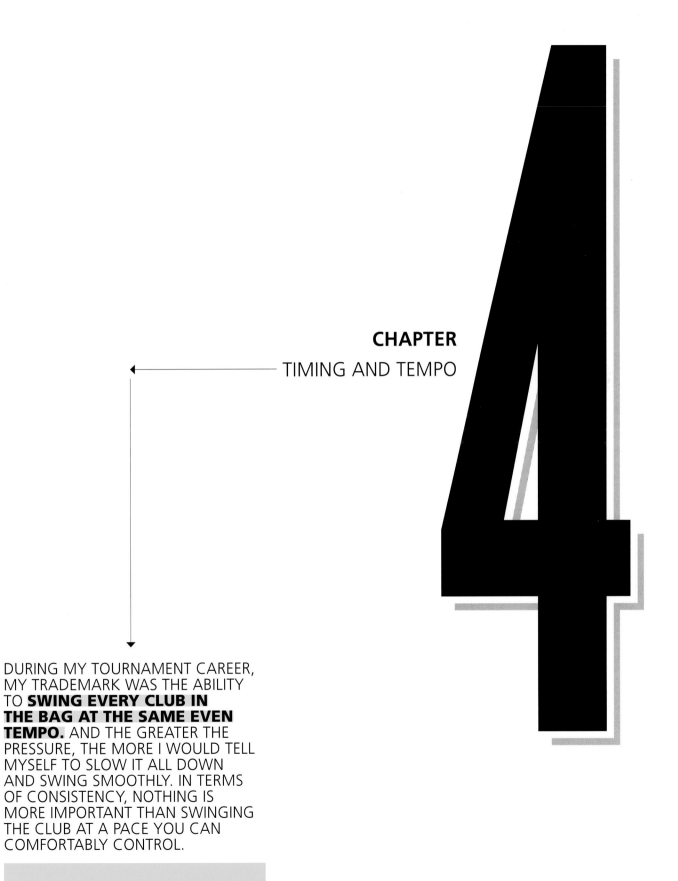

CHAPTER

TIMING AND TEMPO

DURING MY TOURNAMENT CAREER, MY TRADEMARK WAS THE ABILITY TO **SWING EVERY CLUB IN THE BAG AT THE SAME EVEN TEMPO.** AND THE GREATER THE PRESSURE, THE MORE I WOULD TELL MYSELF TO SLOW IT ALL DOWN AND SWING SMOOTHLY. IN TERMS OF CONSISTENCY, NOTHING IS MORE IMPORTANT THAN SWINGING THE CLUB AT A PACE YOU CAN COMFORTABLY CONTROL.

I N THE SPRING of 2000 I enjoyed one of the most memorable experiences of my golfing life when I traveled to The Greenbrier, in the hills of West Virginia, to spend some time in the company of one of the game's true legends, Sam Snead. What started out as a few hours chatting and hitting balls together on the range turned into a weekend-long journey back to the golden era of the game through the eyes of a player regarded the world over as one of the most natural to have ever picked up a club.

It was a privileged audience. Like every successful athlete, Sam knew how to get the most out of his body, and even then, at 88, he swung the club with intuitive grace and balance. I once heard someone describe his rhythm as being "like syrup poured from a tin." Doesn't that conjure a wonderful image? It's one that I have used many times as a means of improving my own rhythm. It was that resonance between body and club that enabled him to generate seemingly effortless power. His footwork was as natural as a ballroom dancer's; he *waltzed* with the golf club, swinging it as though it were a natural extension of his arms and hands. Watching Sam hit balls that weekend was a wonderful reminder to me of the importance not only of a good grip—your physical contact with the club—but also of the quality of your interaction with the ground.

"A good golf swing is all rhythm, and for that you need soft hands," he told me. "The majority of golfers grip the club way too tightly." Whenever Sam was asked about grip pressure, he always used to say that you should grip the club like you would cradle a small bird in your hands—not so tight that you hurt it, but tight enough that it cannot fly away. Those "soft hands" keep the arms and shoulders loose and the clubhead swinging freely. That's the secret

"LIKE SYRUP poured from a tin": Even at 88 years of age, Sam Snead swung the club with enviable grace and rhythm.

to consistency of speed. It's proof that rhythm is one of the secrets to enjoying *A Swing for Life.*

So much of what Sam shared with me over those two days struck a chord with my own thinking. I still have the mini cassette tapes that hold our conversations: pure golfing gold. "The secret to the overall movement is to start the swing right, and by that I mean you have to take it back real smooth and build up speed gradually," he told me in his wonderful West Virginian lilt. "A short, jerky swing never gives you a chance to harness real speed where you need it most—on the ball." The three-time Masters champion also confirmed a view on power hitting that is shared

by Jack Nicklaus: "If I ever needed to put a little heat on it, I would go back even smoother and think about lengthening my turn so as to speed everything up a little bit more," Sam told me. "For a real long one, I'd speed up the turning of the hips through impact—that puts a supercharger on the ball—but the rhythm, the 'oil', must always be there with you." In his heyday, "Slammin' Sam" would lighten up his grip, maximize his turn, and rip through the ball, "pouring on the power with the right side." And things are not so very different out on tour today.

The beauty of Sam's game was that the length of his swing and the speed of the clubhead through the ball were controlled by the athleticism of his body, which is the way I always tried to play. In fact, it's the way I want *you* to play. The better your body action, the more specific you can be in pinpointing an area of focus that can influence ball flight. If I'm looking for maximum distance, for example, I might focus on turning my left shoulder fully under my chin and then pulling with my left shoulder at the start of the downswing to create a "separation" (achieved through pulling my left shoulder away from my chin) before rotating and firing through the ball. With the irons, I might focus on my stomach, using the rotation of my "core" to pace my

swing away from and then toward the target. That's a great thought for a pure, *repeating* rhythm on the approach shots. Thinking about the feeling in your feet and knees—the balance and the energy you take out of the ground—can create powerful messages for your whole body that improve the timing and tempo you enjoy.

YOU HAVE ALL this to discover as you look forward to developing your swing using the drills and exercises featured thus far. I'm now going to add to them my thoughts on how best to instill and maintain good timing and tempo. Above all else, a swinging motion demands that you stay relaxed. And this is where something as simple as breathing correctly can play a big part in your performance, particularly when you're under pressure. Try this basic exercise as you address the ball: Gently breathe out—totally empty your chest—just before you take the club back. As you exhale, you'll feel the tension drain from your body, leaving you with "syrupy" arms and hands that enable you to swing *through* good positions. Keep that in mind in your quest to hone a continuous swinging motion.

Better still, google "Sam Snead swing." Images of him in his prime will inspire you just as they did me.

PAUSE FOR THOUGHT
THE EASIER YOU SWING, THE BETTER YOU'LL HIT IT

I CAN REMEMBER standing on a practice ground discussing the merits of physical effort and the relative quality of my ball-striking with my first coach, Ian Connelly. I'm going back to my early years in the amateur game. Like most headstrong juniors, I always thought I could hit the ball farther than I did. Rather than take a 4-iron, I'd try and hit a hard 5. That aggression through the ball did nothing for my consistency out on the course. Ian suggested a short experiment.

IT WAS ON THE RANGE at Welwyn Garden City that a teenage Nick Faldo developed the rhythm that would become a trademark.

"Take a dozen balls," he said, "and hit six of them as hard as you can with your 5-iron." I did as I was told. "Now, I want you to hit a ball 100 yards—still with your 5-iron. Feel like you're swinging in slow motion. Then increase it to 120 yards, then 140 . . ."

Well, you can guess what happened. The more I eased off, the better I hit the ball and the sweeter it felt coming off the middle of the clubface. When I tried to "smooth" one 160 yards, the ball came off as sweet as a nut and flew farther than the best of the flat-out smashed shots. In that instant, I learned one of the most important lessons in golf, and the ability to swing every club in the bag with a smooth, unhurried rhythm was a trademark throughout my career. Although the shape of my swing has evolved over the years, my tempo—or at least the *consistency* of my tempo—remained a constant.

These days, when I'm coaching a player who's throwing everything at the ball, especially with the driver, I often think back to that discovery I made as a junior and set a challenge: "Okay, now throttle back with a 6-iron and 'chip' me an 80-yarder," I'll say. And then I'll build it up gradually, 20 yards at a time. (You can see where this is going.) By the time I ask the player to "chip me a 100-yard 6-iron," he's nailing it farther than he does with his regular full swing, but he's using half the effort. Keep that in mind the next time you're hitting balls. Throttle all the way back to the smoothest swing you can make, and build your speed gradually. The easier you swing the club, the better you'll strike the ball. Plus, you'll always have a little extra thrust in reserve when you need it.

TEMPO

A PERSONAL CHARACTERISTIC

ONE OF THE many qualities good players share is the discipline to swing the club at an even pace, or *tempo*. If you were to join me on the range at a professional tournament, you'd quickly recognize this consistency of motion all the way through the bag. Some players swing faster than others, which is only to be expected. We all skip to a different beat. But slow or fast, the accomplished golfer has a rhythm, a swing "signature," that runs like a major vein all the way through his game.

Ever since the discovery I made as a junior, I preferred to swing the club with a languid, unhurried tempo. I could hit a few balls with a 3-wood, then drop to a 5-iron, and you would hardly notice the difference in the speed of my body motion or the effort I put into the shot. Trusting the club to do its job, I'd concentrate on making a good turn away from and through the ball. The greater the pressure, the more I would tell myself to *slow it all down*.

One of the most valuable benefits of a swing controlled by the rotary motion of the body is the ability to pace the speed of the arms and hands with the speed of the "core" rotation. Any time I needed to up the ante a little, perhaps to find a little more clubhead speed with a driver, I would focus my energy on pepping up the speed of my hips and stomach as I'd unwind through the ball. Equally, if I wanted to slow it all down, to take something off a shot and fly the ball with the minimum of backspin, I could diminish that rotation. It takes practice, obviously, but with your body and arms working in sync, you can do this without upsetting your rhythm and balance.

The greatest threat to good timing is the urge to physically hit "at" the ball with the hands. On my travels around the world, I don't see many players who swing the club too slowly, but I see plenty who swing it too fast. They have an obvious urge to hammer the ball, and it kills them. Nothing is more effective at exposing latent faults in a golf swing. That's why swinging the club at a speed you can comfortably control is an absolute *must* in my book.

My advice is to watch someone like Luke Donald, a master craftsman who hits every shot in the bag with the same measured, easy rhythm. Nothing is ever hurried; nothing is ever forced. Luke stands out in the modern era as perhaps the finest example of a player who has built his technique around the body-controlled consistency we are looking for and fine-tuned his enviable skills with pure *timing*. A lot of players on tour like to think they swing "within themselves"; Luke defines that quality every time he steps up to the ball, which goes a long way to explaining his ability to control ball flight and spin. What's more, that tempo is the key ingredient that has made Luke one of the finest wedge players and putters on the planet.

Take note: *Consistent through the bag*—that's the message here. Ernie Els has always had that quality in his game. No conversation on rhythm and tempo is ever complete without bringing "the Big Easy" into the equation. Just like Snead in his prime, Ernie has that nonchalant but perfectly synchronized swing that seems to put the ball into orbit. That's the gift of perfect timing. He can fly it 280 yards off the tee all day long, and then—*wallop!*—out of the blue he adds a little more thrust to the hip and "core" rotation through the downswing and puts on another 20 to 30 yards.

When it comes to identifying the tempo that best suits your golf swing, the clues are in the way you walk and the way you talk—the characteristics of simply being *you*. After you identify your personal "beat," make sure you apply it to your whole game. I love to watch K.J. Choi; every move he makes on the course reflects his persona. He's so in tune with how his body works that the pace at which he walks between shots reflects perfectly the tempo with which he then swings the club. With almost military precision, the *turn-turn* motion with which K.J. controls his swing enables him to repeat a tempo that never varies.

In the women's game, I'm equally impressed by Yani Tseng, who goes about her business in the quiet, unassuming fashion that is her trademark on the course. A former junior champion on the Faldo Series, the world No. 1 makes the game look easy because she takes care of the basics and allows her natural tempo to control every aspect of her game.

Of course, it may be that your operating system is a little quicker. We all have a different "twitch factor" of the muscles, and

PLAYING TO A PERSONAL BEAT: The most important thing about your tempo is that it reflects your natural character—and that it is consistent through the bag, as per Luke Donald's example.

identifying your optimum mode is the first step to developing a consistent tempo all the way through the bag. If you're someone who thrives on nervous energy, your swing tempo should reflect that. One of my great contemporaries, Nick Price, always played with a fast, upbeat swing, and it suited his character perfectly.

MY ADVICE TO every player in the early stages of his or her development is to start slowly and build speed as you build confidence. Repetition of good habits is the key, and your senses are more likely to absorb information when you take your time and listen to what your body is telling you. The swing build exercises we looked at in Chapter 3 will gel much more easily if you rehearse them in slow motion and layer them on top of one another, increasing your speed and developing tempo as those feelings become more natural. It's all about

developing "muscle memory." If you focus on swinging the club at a realistic and comfortable pace, your confidence will grow and the links of the chain will slot into place. There's no harm in isolating moves in the swing and working on them to ingrain the feelings associated with good positions, but when it comes to putting it together, you have to focus 100 percent on the overall *flow* of your swing—to keep it well oiled, as Sam Snead would say.

VIDEO LESSON: TEMPO
How do you swing to your own personal beat? Nick Faldo demonstrates a "smoothness" drill that will help you to enjoy a better rhythm and tempo with every club in the bag.

FIND YOUR RHYTHM
A BLEND OF ARMS AND BODY

AT THE START of a warm-up session, your thoughts must be geared toward blending the movement of your arms and hands with the rotation of your body. That is the skill at the heart of a *swinging* motion. And the most effective way to do that is to spend five minutes loosening up your golfing muscles with a few 9-iron shots. Run through that checklist of setup *musts* I gave you: weight on the balls of the feet, flex in the knees, bend from the hips. Then focus on turning your upper body around the spine angle as you encourage your wrists to hinge freely and swing the club up on plane—or in balance, as I like to think about it.

I introduced the concept of swinging the club in balance earlier as a user-friendly way to think about swing plane (more on this in Chapter 8). And there really is a wonderful simplicity to this if you focus on making easy swings with a short iron and listen to what the club tells you. *Rotate and set* to that halfway-back checkpoint, swinging your left arm across your chest and hinging your wrists to turn the club on its end, the shaft cutting through the right shoulder looking down the line. There, it's in *balance,* and the club will feel light in your hands. In making that coordinated move, you've consolidated the vital moving parts that we look for in a sound swing: forearms, wrists, and club all working *together* and in sync with the rotation of the body. The shorter shaft of the 9-iron helps you achieve this, and it does so without you even really having to think about it.

Once I'm satisfied with my basic motion, I turn my attention to repeating an even tempo and controlling the flight of the ball with the length and speed of my body rotation as I work through the bag. You have the heart and soul of your golf swing programmed, and it's now a case of building up speed and momentum in a controlled fashion as you lengthen your swing with the longer-shafted clubs. Ultimately, the purpose of every warm-up session before a game is to establish a rhythm and tempo that produces a consistent ball flight. The better your timing, the more you narrow the gap between your best and worst shots, which in real terms minimizes the damage out on the course.

With the mechanics of my swing in good running order, I could zip through my tournament preparation in just 30 minutes. In fact, from 1992 onward, I had a disciplined routine of hitting four balls with each club, repeating the same even-paced swing on every shot. I'd look for my four shot-shapes: High Fade, Low Fade, High Draw, Low Draw. At the heart of the motion is that rotation of the body, and having turned the dial to tournament speed, I'd finish off with a handful of shots with the 3-wood and driver before coming back to the wedge to begin the process of winding down. That's important. You need a cooling-off period, time to regroup and focus once more purely on rhythm before heading to the tee. I save my distance work with the wedges until the end of a session—when I'm fully warmed up—and spend

AT THE END OF A WARM-UP SESSION, go back to your wedge and challenge yourself to land your first shot 30 yards, the next 35, the next 40, and so on up to your "best" wedge distance with a comfortable full swing. That will fine-tune your rhythm and control.

the last few minutes on distance and trajectory control. A great drill here is to chip a wedge shot 30 yards or so with a real smooth swing and then challenge yourself to land each subsequent ball a handful of yards beyond the previous one. That really does sharpen your feel for the way the arms and body work together as you regulate the length of your swing and the speed of delivery.

DRILL

FOR BETTER ROTATION, SWING WITH FEET TOGETHER

THIS EXERCISE IS as old as the hills, but it's one of the best for capturing the feeling of your body turning and your arms swinging along in harmony. I find it especially useful because it encourages the hips to rotate correctly in the backswing, thus facilitating a good weight shift in tandem with the winding-up of the chest and shoulders. All you need to do is take a 7-iron, stand in good posture with your knees flexed, feet just 8 to 10 inches apart, and then think about making a three-quarter swing with a balanced rhythm. The limited stance automatically encourages the rotation of your hips, which invites the flow of weight into your right knee and thigh as you turn your left shoulder under your chin. In a short time, this exercise encourages you to make a complementary hip and shoulder turn about a steady spine angle—all *musts* in a sound technique.

I see a lot of golfers who make the mistake of restricting their hip rotation a little too much in the belief that doing so will increase the coiling effect as they turn the upper half of their body against that resistance. The danger then is that the swing becomes upper-body dominated to the extent that you lose out on the benefits of a natural and free rotation of the hips (which, remember, must always be made against the stability of that right knee and thigh). Rotating your hips correctly in the backswing not only encourages a better and *fuller* turn of the upper body but also makes it easier to unwind the hips at speed in the recoil. Rory McIlroy provides us with one of the greatest examples in the game today of the way a good hip action benefits the swing generally. So use this exercise as often as you can to add a similar quality to your technique. Not only is swinging a club with your feet together a great warm-up exercise for better rhythm and timing, it can help you free up the hips and "core" area of your body that is so essential to generating speed in the recoil.#

EYES CLOSED HEIGHTENS YOUR SENSES

THE FEELINGS THAT we associate with making a good swing can be dramatically enhanced in slow motion. And even further enhanced if you close your eyes. I've used this technique my whole career. With your eyes shut, you are immediately aware of the way your body works, your "trigger points," and you can use that feedback to determine *exactly* where your tempo originates. Typically, when I do this, I find that my senses are drawn toward my shoulders and lateral muscles in the torso. That's where I feel my swing is controlled. In between hitting shots on the range, I'll often make a point of completing a full shoulder turn with my eyes closed so that I can really let the sensations sink in. With my left shoulder under my chin, my swing feels coiled and "loaded." The muscles in my upper body are stretched like strands of elastic, and I can feel my weight supported on the inside of my right leg.

Rehearsing this exercise on

WHEN YOU LOSE one of your senses, the others sharpen up to compensate—which is why making practice swings with your eyes closed is such a powerful exercise to make yourself aware of the way your swing works and where your tempo originates.

the range or quietly beside the first tee can provide feedback that gives you a real sense of your "control center" and the feelings that gel good motion. What grabs your attention as you wind up the backswing? Do you feel it in your chest? In your knees and hips? Alternatively, try to feel and visualize what the clubface is doing as you rehearse your swing in slow motion, eyes firmly shut. Where is your unwind coming from? Do you stay "connected"—that is, do the arms work in harmony with the torso? There have been many times in my career when I've taken a step

IN THE ROUGH, TAKE IT SMOOTH . . .
Against the resistance of the long grass, you have no choice but to gather speed gradually as you wind and unwind to rip the clubhead through. A great warm-up drill before teeing off.

back and made practice swings with my eyes closed, picturing the way I wanted to work the clubface through the ball, generating the spin that would give me the shape I wanted. I would sometimes imagine there was a small piece of sandpaper on the center of the clubface, and then get a vivid picture in my mind of the way it would zip across the ball. It's incredible how powerful these images can be. Use them to your advantage.

Another valuable source of feedback is the sound you make when you swing the club. Again, this sensation is heightened the moment you close your eyes. Make a few practice swings with

a 3-wood, and listen to the wind whistle off the shaft. The trick is to rotate your body as efficiently as possible with a sense of timing that enables you to translate centrifugal force into clubhead speed as the energy is channeled down through the arms and hands and into the club. Think of spinning a weight on the end of a piece of string—that's the visual to keep in mind when you're looking for speed. Your optimum tempo is that which enables you to build this acceleration gradually, timing the maximum force—and the loudest swish—to coincide with the release through impact.

I always played my best golf with the sense of control coming from *within* my body and stemming directly from the rotation of the core. One of the most effective

ways of connecting with that sensation is to swing a club in thick rough. Against the resistance of the long grass, you have no option but to harness the power within your body to get the club moving smoothly during the initial stages of the backswing; it's impossible to snatch the club away with your hands. Your arms, hands, and stomach (your abs) must work *together* to create the initial momentum that enables you to wind it all up fully before you can even think about ripping through the grass. Try this with your eyes closed, and you'll be left in no doubt as to the importance of utilizing core energy to synchronize that chain reaction we are looking for: a coiling motion that enables you to enjoy maximum acceleration at the bottom of your swing arc.

TEE UP A BALL higher than normal, and with a mid-iron "morph" from your setup into a good impact position—and then try to return to that position for real.

GET OUT OF YOUR OWN WAY FOR SOLID IMPACT

HERE'S A FUN DRILL that not only puts you in touch with what a good impact position feels like but helps you focus on maintaining the "levels" of a good body action that will help you to find and repeat it. Tee up a ball and use a middle iron. Take your setup, and then morph into a good impact position. Feel your hips and chest rotating to the left of the target, weight moving toward your left side, your right knee kicking in gently, your left wrist and forearm braced for the strike. Hold this position for a few seconds, the bottom two grooves on the clubface precisely where you intend them to meet the ball. From here, the key is to move smoothly into your backswing, maintaining your "levels," the equilibrium of your swing, as you wind it all up before returning to this impact position and clipping the ball cleanly off the peg. I used to hit a lot of shots like this on the range, my focus on repeating a rhythm that would allow me to strike the ball precisely and land shots within a tight circle. An even better test is to play into the wind. Strike and trajectory have to be spot on. It's a great way to tune mind and body.#

DRILL

TROUBLESHOOTING
FOCUS ON AREAS OF VULNERABILITY

NINE TIMES OUT of ten, if you sense you might be losing your rhythm out on the course, the problem can be traced to one of two areas: You're too quick and jerky either (1) in the takeaway or (2) during the all-important transition as you reverse momentum at the top of the swing. Those are your two most vulnerable areas. Any tendency to snatch the club away from the ball, or pick the club up (especially for right-side-dominant players), and you're immediately out of sync. Similarly, if you lunge into the downswing and rush your shoulder transition before properly completing the backswing, you'll lose essential "linkage" and continuity of motion between arms and body.

A poor takeaway can often be traced to poor or lazy posture. For instance, your back is too rounded and your shoulders slumped, or you get "flat-footed" and sit back with your weight on your heels. As soon as that happens, the defined structure of a good setup is lost, and your hands and arms are liable to move independently of your body. Your posture simply does not encourage good "linkage" in the swing, and your movements become disjointed.

Remember, the first two or three feet in the backswing—to that 8 o'clock position—must involve the hands, arms, belly, and upper body working *together* to initiate the movement of the club. Only then can you build on early momentum and forge a fluent chain reaction. So, at the first signs of trouble, turn the spotlight on the fundamentals, the *musts* of a good setup position, and double your efforts to create a consensus of motion away from the ball. Focus on your swing trigger, or pressure release. Whatever shape or form it takes, use that cue to inspire a fluent chain of moves from the word "go." Make a positive waggle, shift your weight from side to side, or make a gentle forward press with your hands and wrists. It's up to you to find and practice something—anything!—that triggers a smooth and synchronized movement away from the ball.

Here's one of the reasons golf is such a tough game to master: You can get lazy with your setup and posture even when you're hitting the ball well. I've talked to many great players on this matter, and experience has taught them all the same thing: *You must be ruthlessly disciplined about your pre-shot routine.* At whatever level you play, this is the key to consistency, and it's your greatest ally when you're under pressure. The players who tend to be most successful on tour are those who go through the same motions over and over again, no matter what may be riding on the outcome of a shot. That's what I mean when I talk about true focus and mental strength—the ability to block out what's going on around you and stick to a routine you've rehearsed, a routine you trust.

DRILL

"COLLECT" RHYTHM FROM THE WORD "GO"

A **GOOD RHYTHM IS** not something you stumble across midway through your downswing. Golf just doesn't work that way. In a good swing, that quality has to be seeded the moment the clubhead begins its journey into the backswing, and one of my favorite drills provides just the tonic whenever you feel things may be getting out of sync. Placing a second ball some 12 inches behind (and slightly inside) the one you're aiming to hit sets up the challenge of *collecting* that rear ball as you move through the takeaway before completing your backswing and hitting the shot. The key is that your hands, arms, and stomach work *together* to keep the clubhead low to the ground for the first couple of feet of its journey so you knock that rear ball away. Think about your tempo as you forge those initial links in the chain, collecting the rear ball as you gather momentum. I used to love doing that, and there's no doubt in my mind that this drill helped me to pull off one of the greatest pressure shots in my career. Faced with a 3-iron to the final green in the 1992 Open at Muirfield, I stood over the ball and told myself that all I had to do was "get it away," get the clubhead moving over the first two feet of the swing—if I could just get that early momentum, the chain reaction would take over. Such is the critical importance of the initial moves in the backswing.#

DON'T HURRY, BE HAPPY!

HITTING FROM THE TOP is a problem that affects many golfers—me included!

In 1996 I opened my campaign at Augusta with a Tuesday practice round starting from the 10th . . . and promptly skied my tee shot. Exactly the same thing happened on the 11th. Two pop-ups in the space of twenty minutes. As you might imagine, that gave me plenty to think about as I walked down the fairway into "Amen Corner." As I analyzed the two swings, I realized that on each occasion my "separation" from the top of the backswing had been hurried and way too harsh. I'd made of one of the most common mistakes in golf: swinging too fast from the top.

Right there I reminded myself of the importance of getting my left shoulder under my chin at the top of the backswing before giving myself the green light to unwind. *Complete your backswing turn.* It's one of my *musts*.

The urge to launch yourself into the downswing clearly goes against all we've explored in the dynamic of throwing the gears into reverse, winding and unwinding the swing *from the ground up.* In terms of the overall flow and continuity you enjoy, nothing is more important than your sense of timing as you negotiate this bridge at the start of the downswing. You're aiming for a flawless blending of the two halves that enables your arms and body to unwind in sync, and so generate the most efficient force at impact.

A surefire way to ruin the efficiency of the chain reaction is to drive your legs forward as you start down. So at the first signs of inconsistency in that area, focus on your right knee and "hold it" a moment as you shift into the transition—that is, remain flat-footed on the right foot but still rotate the belly. That's actually a wonderful feeling to have as you settle and re-rotate your hips toward the target; hold that right knee a split second, stay on that right foot a fraction longer, and then "fire" and release the whole of your right side through impact. Now's a good time to draw on any key thoughts you've identified in the swing build to reinforce those feelings of a smooth transition: *slow and unwind.* Give yourself the luxury of time, and good things will happen.

One of the most effective drills I relied on for many years involved splitting my stance: drawing my left foot back until the toe of the shoe was level with the right heel. When my feet were so

placed, any tendency I might have had to slide my knees toward the target at the start of the downswing was soon history. Try it, and I guarantee you'll find that the legs can do nothing but support the rotary motion of your body as you settle and unwind through that all-important transition. Go ahead and hit as many balls as you can with your feet in this position. You'll develop a wonderful sense of timing at the top of your swing as you "settle" and then re-rotate in the downswing. There is no leg-drive to disrupt the sequence, just a lovely sense of the muscles in your torso stretching like strong elastic as you coil your upper body and then a natural recoil down

and through the ball. Wait for your moment—pause at the top—and then release your whole right side through impact. Tee up a ball and hit as many shots as you can with this drill—it can only do you good.

Another fix that can come in handy on the course during a round is simply to turn your driver around, grip the head, and swing the shaft. You won't make a positive swish until you unwind in a sequence that allows you to build acceleration gradually, so this is always a good test. Make a full windup and full stretch, but swing smoothly—feel your tempo come from *within* your body—and make the wind whistle.#

THROUGH THE BAG
ONE SWING FITS ALL

MANY GOLFERS ASK me how they should adjust their swing to accommodate the different lofts and lie angles between clubs. It's a perfectly reasonable question, but not something you need to worry unduly about. The beauty of the concept that we're working on is that controlling your swing with the rotation of your body relies purely on the quality of your setup position. That is your priority on every shot. As long as your clubs have been built to suit your needs as an individual—and being professionally "custom-fit" is a *must* for any serious player—your only concerns should be setting up to the ball correctly, as per the details we looked at in "The Fundamentals" (Chapter 2), and then winding and unwinding your body (playing to that personal "beat") as you turn back and through toward the target.

Trajectory and shot shape will vary, but the basic swing thoughts are the same whether you're using a driver, a 6-iron, or a 9-iron. As the length of the shaft increases, your posture adjusts accordingly (that is, you stand a little taller with a 6-iron than you do with a 9-iron), and the plane of the swing automatically flattens out the longer the club you happen to be using. Again, this isn't something you consciously need to think about. On every full swing, your job is simply to *complete* your shoulder turn around the spine angle created at the setup and to synchronize the moving parts with the quality of your wrist-and-forearm action. Let physics take care of the details. With the longer irons and woods, your shoulders turn progressively further than your chest, your chest further than your hips, and your hips further than your knees—the logical sequencing of a dynamic body action. The longer the shaft of the club, the longer the swing arc and, as momentum builds, the greater the clubhead speed through the ball.

I'm often asked where and when the full "setting" of the wrists occurs in the backswing, and there are no hard-and-fast rules here to live by. Over the years, as my game and my understanding of the swing evolved, I used the timing of that full wrist set to influence the type of shot I wanted to play. Although the framework of my body action remained consistent, I experimented with the timing of the wrist set and its effect on the delivery of the club in the downswing. For example, the more I wanted to "trap" the ball with a downward strike for backspin (with the short irons), the earlier I would look for that setting in the backswing. Moving to the other end of the scale, the driver is the most obvious candidate for experimentation with a later set as you search for width and speed, the full and final setting in the wrists occurring as the momentum of the clubhead pulls them into position at the very top of the swing.

We could fill an entire book identifying all of the specific changes in body angle, hip rotation, swing arc, and clubhead speed between all of the different clubs in the bag, a process that would provide you with absolutely nothing tangible and meaningful to focus on. All I have ever been interested in was making a swing that revolved around those fundamentals, in which the dynamics of a sound body motion could be seen to be at the heart of a natural, repeating *swing*. And surely that's your goal, too.

9-IRON

6-IRON

DRIVER

THE ULTIMATE TEST FOR BALANCED BALL-STRIKING

WORKING AROUND THE assumption that only a "quiet" leg action will give you any chance of repeating a sound swing, you'll find there's no greater test of your balance and the controlled synchronization of your arms and body than hitting full iron shots off sand. Any time you have access to a practice bunker, take the opportunity to put your rhythm to the test. Don't shuffle your shoes into the sand, as you would to play a regular greenside sand shot. Imagine you're standing on eggshells as you assume a

good posture and balance your weight evenly between your feet. Swaying off the ball and losing your height (your "levels") is simply not an option if you're going to pick the shot cleanly, so your focus here is on controlling and stabilizing your swing with a passive leg action. On such a delicate footing, the only way you can hope to re-lease the club at a consistent depth is to blend arm swing with body rotation—and to pace your overall motion with a chilled rhythm. When I do this, I focus on the rotation of my middle, and I feel my arms freewheel in response as I unwind to face the target. Any attempt to rush into the swing, or hurry the transition, and you're liable to catch the shot "fat," taking a divot of sand. Question is, how many clean shots can you hit in succession?#

1992 *Shaping up to the challenges of Muirfield, Open Championship*

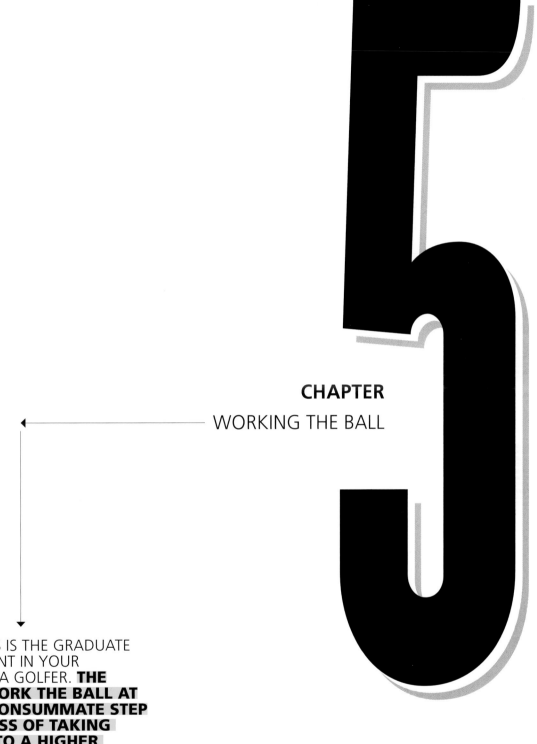

CHAPTER

WORKING THE BALL

SHAPING SHOTS IS THE GRADUATE
SCHOOL ELEMENT IN YOUR
EDUCATION AS A GOLFER. **THE
ABILITY TO WORK THE BALL AT
WILL IS THE CONSUMMATE STEP
IN THE PROCESS OF TAKING
YOUR GAME TO A HIGHER
LEVEL.** IT'S THE KEY TO PLOTTING
STRATEGY AND COPING WITH THE
SPECIAL DEMANDS OF THE WIND.

TAKE A MINUTE to really study this image of Ben Hogan,* just moments before impact. A similar photograph had a profound effect on my own understanding of the golf swing, and this one can help you, too. There is a calmness about the position that tells you he was in total control over the way the club was to be delivered and *released* through the ball—to influence the flight with a fade or a draw, to send it up high or keep it low. To me, this captures the essence of shot-making. The whole idea of working on a consistent backswing position and taking such care through the transition is that you enter this zone of control on the way down to the ball; there is a feeling that you have all the time in the world to *release* the clubhead in a way that ties in perfectly with your visual image of the flight and result of the shot.

You can rotate the forearms over each other, or "hold it off," retaining the angle in your right wrist and thus denying the clubface the opportunity to rotate over the ball. Whatever you need to do to *shape* the shot the way you see it. Better players will understand exactly what I mean when I say there's nothing better than the feeling of the forearms being in this "slot" approaching impact, swinging the club from a natural inside path, with the wrists still "loaded," just waiting for the moment of truth—impact.

Through the process of the swing-build thus far, my hope is that I have at least helped you develop a concept of the way a repeating swing revolves around a consistent body action—one that enables you to swing the arms and club in harmony. You need that *togetherness* and "connection" of arms and body before you can begin to think about shaping shots. You also need to recalibrate your understanding of impact, so that you have in your mind's eye a clear vision of this organic series of movements, starting a foot or so ahead of the ball and extending all the way to the finish. Think about impact as *being* impact, and the danger is that your swing effectively stops there, neglecting the critical motion *through the ball*. We talked about this briefly in Chapter 3, and the full significance of this more sophisticated style of thinking will help you recognize the feelings involved with manipulating the path and position of the clubface all the way through that impact channel or play zone in order to influence the ball flight.

The renaissance of my career in the mid-1980s was built around the security of a bulletproof body action within which my arms and hands were very much *alive* in the business of swinging the clubhead. *Feel within a framework*— that was the secret to my success. Shaping shots, banking the ball against a wind, picturing a certain trajectory to attack a pin—this is playing golf. It's extremely rare that a top player will visualize and attempt to play a dead-straight shot to a target. If I were holding a ball against a slight crosswind with either a fade or a draw, then yes, I might see a straight shot with the shorter clubs. Otherwise there is always movement, whether that's your natural ball flight or an accentuated spin. And the key is that you always respond to a positive picture in your mind.

If I want to peel in a gentle fade, the feeling is all in the right wrist and forearm. I would set the angle in the right wrist on the way back and then maintain it all the way through. A draw? I let the right

*AS FOR HOGAN'S "SECRET"?
Cupping the left wrist on the way back might well have had something to do with it. That is such a nice feeling to have, working the left arm in close harmony with the chest so that as you unwind, you have that wonderful control over the delivery of the clubhead. For me, the cupping action guarantees the clubface is not shut on the way down; it works from a neutral position—that is, the angle of the clubface is in tune with your own thoughts as you unwind toward the ball. Having said that, I was once told the "secret" was the speed of the right knee through impact—so perhaps the only conclusion we can draw with any certainty is that this is a mystery that will run and run!

wrist and forearm rotate freely through the impact area, turning the toe end of the clubface over the heel.

When I give clinics to the talented juniors who play on the Faldo Series each season, I make a point of underlining the art of visualization—*playing to the picture,* as I call it. Kids are especially receptive to imagery, copying, and mimicking, which are some of the most powerful tools of learning. I might demonstrate throwing a ball high over a tree— and then ask a player to translate that action into a golf swing. And sure enough, they make a natural move in which the body hangs back to allow for a full release of the arms that slides the clubhead

under the ball, hoisting it high into the sky. If I throw a low ball to demonstrate staying ahead of a shot, that same action is interpreted in a controlled swing that punches the ball low.

Body language plays a huge part in all of the shots we're about to explore, and the nature of the release is reflected in the shape of the follow-through position with each of them. The human brain is so powerful, and you want to harness every facet of its capability to help you play good golf, whether that is in feelings and sensations associated with certain swing positions or—as we move into the realm of shot-making—in the way you *see* the flight of the ball and translate those images into technique. As I say, *playing to the picture.*

PAUSE FOR THOUGHT

A GOLF LESSON FROM JACK . . .

PLAYING IN THE San Diego Open at Torrey Pines in 1982, I found myself in the company of a rampant Jack Nicklaus and big-hitting Andy Bean. Between them, they ripped the course apart, Nicklaus signing for a superb 64 and Bean a 68. I shot a lackluster 71, which at the time felt more like 81. Later that evening I found myself analyzing Jack's round. I had been treated to a display of near-perfect ball-striking. A tough pin location was no obstacle; Jack's iron shots tore off at the middle of the green before leaning one way or the other to seek out the flag, as if guided by radar. If the pin was cut to the right, his shots tipped obediently to the right. If the pin was tucked left, his shots tapered left. This was Nicklaus doing what Nicklaus did best: thinking his way around a course and working the ball to order. He never looked like he would miss a green. On the odd occasion he caught one of his irons a little too "flush," he might end up in the heart of the green, leaving a 20-foot birdie putt instead of the usual 5-footer. A 64 was the worst score he could do that day.

That experience had a profound effect on my decision to change my swing. If I wanted to be one of the best players in the world, I needed the versatility to work the ball both ways. Just like Jack.

SHAPE YOUR SHOTS
INCREASE YOUR MARGIN FOR ERROR

OVER THE YEARS many people accused me of being an overly mechanical player. But how little they know. Within the framework of a reliable body movement, my entire game from tee to green was based on my ability to manipulate the trajectory of my shots with a subtle hand-and-forearm action through impact. To play good golf, you need educated hands and forearms, and the ideas that I'm about to share will set you on the road to understanding the basic principles of swing path and ball flight. Ultimately, of course, the most valuable lessons here revolve around the feedback you experience on the practice tee.

It hardly needs to be said that spinning the ball is an advanced technique. But when you get to the stage where your swing is in *sync,* when your arm-swing complements a good body movement, you can begin to think about the nature of impact and experiment with the way you release the clubhead. Of course, working the ball isn't just about your ability to create spin deliberately. Every player has a *natural* shape of shot. As you begin to strike the ball more consistently, you'll find that you tend to have a shape that flies gently either right to left or left to right—that is, a draw or a fade. That dominant shape is the style you must base your game around. That's your "go-to" shot, the natural shape that you will always have the best chance of pulling off.

My own preference was always a fade, a gentle movement from left to right, maybe as little as five feet in the air. It's the shape I feel most comfortable playing, so wherever possible that's the shot I instinctively look for on the course. But your natural spin doesn't always fit the bill. As your skill level develops, you'll start to think more in terms of attacking the pin (not just hitting the green), and then you'll discover the real challenge of working the ball. You need the ability to shape your shots in either direction so that every pin is accessible.

If the pin is cut toward the back left corner of a green, my thoughts generally would be to fire a shot at the middle of the green with a draw. On the other hand, if I face a shot to a flag cut tight behind a bunker in the front right quarter of a green, I play a fade. In both cases, I aim for the fat of the green and let the ball work toward the pin. On a good ball-striking day, that deviation through the air may be as little as 5 to 15 feet—but you have that margin for error built in. That's the key. Just as Nicklaus demonstrated so beautifully all those years ago, the smart shot is the one that errs on the side of caution. What you don't want to do on approach shots is short-side yourself, which means missing a green right when the pin is cut to the right, or left when the pin is on the left.

In any sort of wind, the plot thickens.

Picture an approach of 165 yards—something on the order of a 7-iron. There's a breeze blowing from the right, and the pin is cut tight on the right side of the green. The only way to land and stop the ball close to the hole is to neutralize the effect of the wind with counter-spin—in this case a fade. Aiming dead on the flag, I would try to make a punchy, three-quarter swing, and pull the clubface across the ball (holding the angle in the right wrist) to fashion a shot that holds its line with a subtle left-to-right spin. To the naked eye, the ball appears to be flying dead straight. The reality is that the ball is spinning from left to right just to hold its own in the crosswind.

STUCK IN A similar situation, the one-way right-to-left player finds himself in trouble. He is forced to aim away to the right of target and ride the wind to bring the ball back. He has no real control of landing distance or spin. As the ball reaches the apex of its flight and turns toward the pin, it is actually sailing *downwind* and so is unlikely to settle on the green.

Clearly, having the ability to control spin opens up a whole new ball game. In many cases, gently curving the ball through the air also widens your margin for error. Think about your strategy off the tee. If your normal shot shape is a fade, the optimal play is to aim down the left side of the fairway and let the ball work its way back toward the middle. Play to your strengths. That way, you effectively increase your landing area—you have the whole width of the fairway to land your ball.

To take a different angle, working the ball can also be your best line of defense under pressure. I often find myself in a position

where I simply cannot afford to have the ball leak left or right, and so I think about blocking out one side of the course. A classic example would be the second shot to the 11th at Augusta. With water lurking on the left side of the green—and room to the right—my first thought is that I don't want to hit a shot with right-to-left spin. My approach to No. 11 was always a fade, a shot that does all it can to work away from the hazard. (In this sort of situation I would slightly increase grip pressure in the last two fingers on my left hand; that's always a good anti-left measure!)

THERE'S NO SHORTAGE of opportunity here. I'm going to explain to you in detail the thoughts and feelings that I associate with a shot-shaping system I always refer to as *one backswing, four follow-throughs*. My favorite techniques for hitting a fade and a draw originate from the same stock backswing, whereupon the feel that I have as I deliver the club through the impact area produces one of four distinct outcomes: two types of left-to-right shots, and

two right-to-left. Pay particular attention to the nature of the finish; pick up on the body language and develop that into feelings of your own. (You may discover that these four shots with the same club fly the ball slightly different distances, so it's well worth taking note of exact yardages in each case. How many times in a round do you get a "stock" yardage?)

OF COURSE, THERE are times when you do have the luxury of choosing your preferred shot, and working the ball to escape trouble is the other focus of this chapter. You need the ability to bend shots quite dramatically to negotiate trees, and the technique here, which basically involves offsetting the alignment of your swing with the angle of the clubface, is much easier to grasp. We'll come to that a little later. First, let's look at the fade and the draw.

ADVANCED TECHNIQUE: THE FALDO FADE

HOLD OFF THE CLUBFACE

WORKING THE BALL is all about matching certain feelings to the images you see in your mind. With the security of a consistent posture and setup position, I simply picture the shot shape that I want to play and *feel* the desired spin in my forearms and hands as I swing the clubhead through the impact area—that play zone I talked about earlier—extending all the way to the finish. From midway in the downswing all the way to the conclusion of the follow-through, you conjure the necessary formula to generate spin.

My favorite shot was always the fade, which involves *holding off* the clubface to impart left-to-right spin on the ball, which might only move a few feet in the air. This was my stock shot through the best years of my career, and the feeling that I relied on to execute it came almost entirely from my right wrist. In the course of making the backswing, I would *set* the right wrist as normal, and then focus on maintaining that angle

at the back of the wrist all the way through impact as I rotated my body to the finish. *The right wrist does not release*—that was my feeling. The reality was that I would still release the club on the way

to the finish, but that release was delayed sufficiently to prevent the toe passing the heel, thus creating left-to-right spin. It's a sensation, more than anything; and that feeling is enough to produce a slight *tip* fade, the ball reaching the apex of its flight before gently falling to the right.

A satisfying shot, and one that *never* goes left.

We call this technique the *hold-off* for the way in which you literally hold off the release, doing all you can to prevent the toe of the clubface from turning over the heel, as it would normally do. The sensation you're looking for is that of your hips and shoulders turning and working faster than the club-head through impact, so your arms follow suit and swing hard to the left, pulling the clubface across the ball. I like to imagine there's a piece of sandpaper on the clubface, and I pull it across the ball to simulate the amount of sidespin I'm looking for: gently for a slight fade, hard and fast for a real worker against the wind or to shape a shot around a bunker.

Such intuitive shot-making takes time and patience to master, but the more you experiment, the more you will learn from the feedback you get. Rotate your left forearm and set your wrists to make your backswing (as normal), and then hold that angle in the right wrist as you unwind, squeezing just a tad more firmly with the left hand. Grip a little more firmly in the last three fingers of your left hand. That encourages a firm left wrist through impact, and you can go aggressively at it. For a mega hold-off, the key is to keep the club as high as possible coming in to impact—you really do hold the angle in the wrists for an extra-late hit. A great way to develop this technique is to hit balls on a steep downhill lie, as you are forced to keep the club high to avoid catching the ground before the ball and hitting the shot fat. Practicing in this fashion will teach you to lead with the heel of the iron. In fact, out on the course, when I'm looking for a severe hold-off, I'll often say to myself "Get the heel there first," and then power through with my right shoulder.

Characteristic of this technique is the follow-through position, specifically the behavior of the left arm as it climbs into the finish. See how the left elbow works out and up as my hands and arms lead the clubhead. Depending on how severely I hold off the release in this fashion, I can move the ball up to 20 feet or so through the air, which brings me to the *chicken wing,* and one of the best manufactured pressure shots of my career.

EXAGGERATE THE FEELING OF *WINGING* IT . . .

HAVING LED BY four shots entering the final round, I found myself standing in the 15th fairway at Muirfield in the 1992 British Open trailing by one and with a problem on my hands. A good drive into a gusting right-to-left wind had left me with 165 yards to a pin that was located in the front right-hand corner of the green, just beneath a ridge. Time was running out, and I knew I needed a birdie. The *chicken wing* I hit in there with a 5-iron held up against the wind and finished inside four feet. In a sense it was a shot that defined all that I had worked for—the ability to control ball flight when I absolutely needed to in the biggest championship in the world. Just as I pictured it, I fed the ball into the slope and it settled down right next to the hole.

I call this shot the *chicken wing* because of the way it exaggerates that left arm action into the finish, really *breaking* the left elbow so the clubface has absolutely no chance of rolling over. Photo-

graphs can never quite capture the feelings involved, but there is a huge difference between the release to play a regular fade and my *wing*. It's almost a professional block, a cover drive in cricket. It is *guaranteed* to keep the ball working from left to right, a slide. It's a shot that has saved

me on more than one occasion. I would aim down the left side of the green, or the left side of the fairway, and let the ball work back toward the target. In the wind I always try to make it a *soft-arm* version—in fact, I'd suggest that's a good swing thought for any sort of windy conditions. You can be super-aggressive with this technique, too, enjoying total freedom as you unwind through the ball.

ADVANCED TECHNIQUE: THE FALDO DRAW

A NATURAL RELEASE ON THE INSIDE PATH

WITHOUT MAKING any conscious adjustment to my setup position, I quieted my body rotation and encouraged the natural release of the forearms to play a draw, a gentle shot that curves from right to left through the air. I work on rotating my left forearm away from the ball just as I normally would to make my backswing, but this time focusing on re-rotating my left arm through impact and at the same time letting the right wrist release,

straightening the back of the right wrist after impact. The result is that the clubface turns over the ball to create that right-to-left spin.

If this all sounds complicated, stop a minute and simply compare this sequence of images with those illustrating the fade on the previous pages. The differences are clear. To induce that right-to-

left spin, you must encourage the rotation of the forearms in the direction of the target, so that you enjoy a more rounded angle of attack. Feel it as you release your hands and arms. This time you want the toe end of the club to turn over the heel, so the clubface imparts that right-to-left spin on the ball.

The interesting thing here is that when I think about the rotation of the arms, I focus on it coming from the upper part of

my arms—the triceps. This makes for a gearing effect as the influence of that rotation filters all the way down through my forearms and hands into the club itself. In a sense, this diminishes the influence of that rotation, but it also makes it a lot safer and easier to control. The hands and wrists are a little too close to the real action, and so the danger in focusing your attention there is that you can overcook it. As a means of fine-tuning your control, focus instead on rotating your triceps. The fact that they can't over-rotate is in your favor—your *max* will never be too much.

Every picture tells a story: When you're playing a fade, the restricted, held-off finish perfectly matches the intention to cut across the ball and spin it from left to right. By comparison, the fuller and flatter "wraparound" position you arrive at playing a draw is the natural conclusion to rolling the clubface over the ball when the emphasis is on spinning a shot from right to left. It's a subtle but telling difference. We're talking about fractional manipulation of the clubface, which is all it takes to spin a golf ball. Identifying with this body language will help you to go out and experience for real the special relationships between the follow-through position and your intention to shape the ball with these highly effective shots.

THINK "ROTATE-ROTATE" FOR THE SUPER DRAW

THE REGULAR draw swing might give me five to eight yards of movement through the air. Whenever I needed to shape it a little more dramatically right-to-left, I'd call on my "rotate-rotate" swing, really cranking up the sensation of rotating the upper arms and wrapping the arms low around my body at the finish. To play this shot, I would also move the ball back a touch and make a conscious effort to turn my shoulders fully—this is very much a shoulder-controlled motion, the arms transferring this influence to the clubface. Again, my attention is on rotating the triceps in sync with the shoulders. With my lower body relatively quiet, this enables me to turn the ball the length of maybe half a green, perhaps a touch more. So

if the pin is tucked in behind a left-hand bunker, the ball is actually coming in around the corner. This really is an attacking shot that comes in at a completely different angle. It's a useful shot to have in a hard left-to-right wind. Flighting a shot with extreme draw keeps the trajectory down, which you can further accentuate the softer you keep the arms. As you release the club, you want to develop that feeling of the right forearm chasing after the ball.

VIDEO LESSON:
TRACKMAN DRAW VERSUS FADE Using TrackMan analysis, Nick Faldo explains the basic principles behind the adjustments in technique required to manipulate ball flight with a draw and a fade.

DON'T FIGHT THE WIND!

BUNT IT LOW WITH SOFT ARMS

VIDEO LESSON:
THE KNOCKDOWN SHOT
Softening the arms and
shortening the follow-
through enables you to
take spin off the ball and
lower the trajectory—
perfect for those blus-
tery links conditions!

IN MY PREPARATION for links golf, I always loved to experiment with different ways of taking spin off the ball to lower trajectory and generally add to my control. When I was playing in the 1992 U.S. Open at Pebble Beach, the wind blew so hard off the Pacific Ocean that I spent a lot of time working on what I describe as a soft-arms, *bunty* type of shot, taking all of the aggression out of impact and flying the

ball with a minimum amount of spin. To the naked eye, you aren't going to see too much of a difference between this and a regular draw swing, but you will certainly feel it, and the telltale follow-through again reflects the nature of the shot. On a scale of 1 to 10, this is a 7 for effort. I'm swinging

totally within myself, the arms swinging close to the body both on the way back and through the ball. The commitment here is to let the right wrist go and rotate the right forearm after the ball all the way to the finish, keeping the arms and shoulders *soft* all the way. A fun image is to try and put your right thumb into your left ear on the follow-through! Swing easy, hit it solid, and fly it low, under the radar.

PRESET SPIN
SLING IT, SLIDE IT TO GET OUT OF JAIL

THE IDEAS THAT I have shared thus far are fairly advanced techniques, used to neutralize the effect of the wind, or to shape a shot to a flag or a certain tee shot. This is the *feel* in me, creating four different follow-throughs from that standard backswing position. But there is a limit to the degree to which you can spin the ball like this. When you really need to bend the ball more severely, you have to think in terms of offsetting the alignment of your body and your swing with the alignment of the clubface. This is all about applying a straight edge to a radius, and the basic technique that I was taught as a junior can pave the way for you to develop your sense of control.

SLIDING IT LEFT TO RIGHT

TO MAKE THE ball spin left to right, aim the leading edge of the clubface at the point where you want the ball to finish, then adjust your body alignment until your hips, knees, and shoulders are open in relation to your target. Position the ball in the forward part of your stance, and spread your weight evenly between your feet.

Now for the simple part: *Once you have built in the necessary adjustments, you are free to make your regular swing.* It's like playing a golf computer game. You select the alignment of the clubface first, then offset the alignment of your body before hitting the "play" button. To do this correctly, align the clubface just holding the grip loosely, and then, once you've assumed your stance—aiming your body line either to the left or right of target—regrip the club in the normal way. In the final analysis, your grip matches your shoulder alignment. And with the angle of the clubface and the alignment of your body now effectively at odds, you have preset the formula required to make the ball spin. Here, with a 4-iron, the ball will start on the line of my body before the slice spin takes over and it soars toward the target. The more spin you need, the more you offset the clubface to your body alignment (and the less loft you would use, giving you a straighter face to play with). The *slice factor* is thus increased. If you feel it's necessary, you can further increase the left-to-right spin by holding off the clubface—adding a *feel* element.

Go out and experiment and have some fun with this. It's one of the most useful recovery shots in golf. Just keep in mind that it is very hard to generate significant sidespin with anything less than a 6- or 7-iron. The more loft, the more backspin you create, which overrides sidespin. Just another thought to keep in your locker.

RIGHT-TO-LEFT SLINGSHOT

NO SURPRISES HERE: You make the opposite pre-swing adjustments to play a raking right-to-left draw. Aim the clubface directly on your target, but this time get your body in a closed position—that is, your feet, hips, and shoulders all traveling *right* of your aim point. That closed stance relative to your target line gives you a terrific feeling of turning and swinging in a circular motion. Your thoughts should be on rotating the clubface through impact. Try to make the toe-end of the clubface turn over the heel, and *close the gate* on the ball. Commit yourself to releasing the entire right side of your body and *chase* the ball with your right shoulder to a flat finish, hands low around your neck. In other words, encourage your body language to underline the shape you're looking for.

The mechanics involved in playing this extreme draw naturally de-loft the clubface, so expect the ball to fly a little lower than normal, and allow for some extra run. Take at least one less club than you normally would from the fairway, and aim to run the ball onto the front of a green.

Curving the ball right to left is generally the easier of the two shots for the right-handed player, and as you become more confident, you can really stretch this offset principle to its limits to produce a boomerang hook. Find a location that enables you to practice slinging shots around an obstacle, whether it's a tree or a bush, and experiment with the ball position, moving the ball forward for extra height, further back in the stance for a lower, punchier, trajectory. Adjustments to your grip can make a difference, too. Strengthening both the left and right hands will help you to rotate further and *release* the clubhead for hook spin (a weaker grip will neutralize the face for a slice).

HIGH AND LOW? PLAY TO THE PICTURE

LET'S FINALLY TURN our attention to the highs and lows of shot-making. Suppose you have a shot of 140 yards or so, and a tall tree is blocking your line. There is no way you can go around the tree and still have your ball hold the green, while the option to play beneath the branches simply does not exist. You have to go over the tree.

Typically, a shot of this distance would call for a 9-iron, but I would take an 8-iron and move the ball forward in my stance, which is open to the target line. With the emphasis on maximizing upward momentum through the ball, I'd then let my weight favor my right side while my hands find a comfortable position just behind the ball. A light grip pressure keeps the hands and forearms relaxed, and you want them to be active with this shot, so they can accelerate freely. These adjustments effectively *add* loft to the clubface, and there should be a feeling of being physically *behind* the shot.

With a positive visual of the ball climbing steeply and clearing the top of the tree, I then make a full swing and focus on sliding the face cleanly underneath the ball—you're not looking to compress down and take much of a divot here. The feeling you're after is one of releasing the angle in the right arm much earlier—feel the right hand swing away from the right shoulder as you start down—so that you're able to catch the ball on the very bottom groove on the clubface, fractionally on the upswing. There isn't much in the way of weight shift here; stay behind on your right side as you unwind to shallow out your swing arc.

The sum of all I have described above adds loft to the clubface and gives you the sensation of hoisting the ball into the air. Test yourself while practicing to see how high you can hit all of your irons. As you will discover, this shot naturally flies from left to right, so make a note to factor that in whenever you encounter this sort of situation on the course.

For many amateurs, the low punch shot is the harder of the two extremes. The problem, I think, is often a tendency to want to play the ball too far back in the stance, and lean the weight heavily onto the left side, which automatically creates a steep swing. I see a lot of players reach for a 3- or 4-iron, then move the ball back to a position inside the

right heel and push their hands forward. The 3-iron is now looking like a 1-iron. Even before attempting to play the shot, they've smothered the ball.

So make club selection your first consideration. A 4- or 5-iron will usually do the job, because by the time I have finalized my setup, with the ball just back of center and my hands eased gently forward, the natural loft is greatly reduced, *but still playable.* To enhance my feel and control for the shot, I usually choke down the grip, and my weight is favoring my left side.

What you are looking at now is basically a good impact position.

This is where you want to return to, rotating your upper body so that you *cover* the ball with your torso as you unwind, close down the loft, and cut short the release. I make the backswing just as I normally would, with thoughts of *rotate and set,* then commit to pulling down and through with my left side as my upper body rotates toward the target. The secret here is that your body is moving and rotating ahead of the club. The hands lead the clubface through the ball, and as the face is de-lofted, the shot is knocked down. The restricted follow-through is purely evidence of the fact that your intention is to *bunt*

the ball forward. And remember: The harder you swing, the more spin you create and the higher the ball will fly. So stick with an easy tempo, swing easy, and control the trajectory.

On any punch shot I always like to feel like my pressure is right in the middle of the grip—neither hand has more control than the other. Discoveries like this often surprise you. If you want to increase speed, you have to increase the tempo of your rotation, but I also think about adding acceleration with the elbows. If the elbows are moving fast, then the hands will be, too, with the benefit of being fully under control.

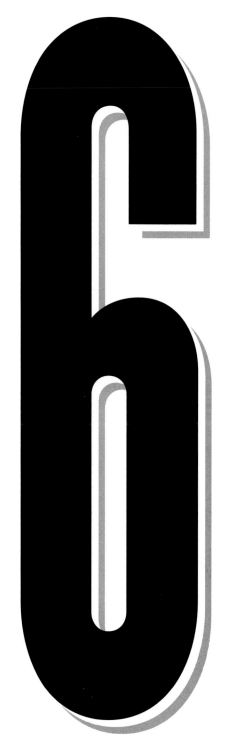

CHAPTER

A DRIVING LESSON

YOU DON'T CHANGE YOUR GOLF SWING WITH A DRIVER—YOU SIMPLY HAVE TO MAKE IT BETTER, FASTER, AND MORE EFFICIENT TO MAXIMIZE YOUR DISTANCE OFF THE TEE.

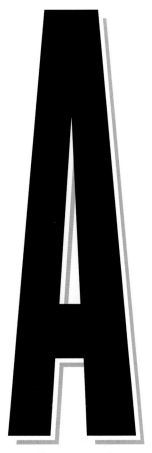

S THE DEFENDING champion at the 1997 Masters, I enjoyed the privilege of placing the green jacket on the shoulders of the new champion, Tiger Woods. And what a champion. After all the hype and speculation surrounding the arrival of golf's new *wunderkind,* the performance he put together under the spotlight that week was extraordinary on a number of levels, but perhaps most impressive was his unshakable maturity inside the ropes. We had been paired together for the opening round, and there was no doubt in my mind that I had been treated to a glimpse of golf's future superstar.

The speed with which Tiger tore through the ball was just phenomenal, the guided missiles he launched off the tee followed by towering iron shots to the greens. His game could have been built for Augusta National. With a near-flawless demonstration of controlled power golf, the 21-year-old became the youngest Masters champion ever, winning by 12 shots with an 18-under-par total of 270. These are still records today.

Only time will tell whether or not Tiger succeeds in his quest to surpass Jack Nicklaus as golf's most prolific major winner, but one thing is certain: The fundamental nature of the game was changed forever as a result of that historic victory. Tiger raised the bar in every department. "Athleticism" emerged as the new buzzword in golf's lexicon, as players, coaches, and commentators tried to make sense of what they had just seen. The sheer physicality and dynamic motion of Tiger's swing made everyone take notice—while the stats told their own sobering story. Tiger's average driving distance that week was 323 yards—25 yards ahead of his nearest rival. The longest club he hit into a par 4 was a 7-iron, and on at least two occasions he reduced the par-5 15th hole to a driver and a wedge. One of the most astonishing performances ever witnessed in the history of the game signaled the dawn of a new era. Suddenly, at the highest level, golf was all about speed and power.*

After 20 years on tour, my playing career was well into its back nine just as Tiger was blazing a trail for the next generation, but along with everyone else, I found myself analyzing his technique and hoping I might find a few precious extra yards. I've always thought that you don't change your swing with a driver, you simply have to make it better and more efficient in order to maximize distance. What struck me most was the efficiency of Tiger's body action, the gradual gathering of pace as he wound up like a spring, creating width in a compact backswing before firing with that tremendous "flash-speed" through the ball. (Oh, to be 21 again!) I was certainly not alone in tailoring my workouts to focus on the muscle groups that control the rotational speed of the hips and abdomen, and my advice to the serious golfer is to seek the assistance of a qualified physical trainer who can help you target "golf-specific" exercises designed to improve flexibility and strengthen your core.

Professional guidance is also a *must* when it comes to taking full advantage of the latest technology out there to help you make the most effective use of whatever speed potential you have. I'm talking here about the benefits of getting your equipment properly "custom-fit" so that the shaft and loft of the driver you are hold-

*To put Tiger's numbers into some sort of perspective, when I won my third Masters title, in 1996, my driving average was 267 yards. Working backward from green to tee, I geared my strategy toward positional play. I wanted the best angle to attack a flag, and if a par 5 was out of reach in two shots, I would lay up to a favorite pitching distance. In that Sunday duel with Greg Norman I can remember agonizing over my second shot at the No. 13—was it a 2-iron or a 5-wood? I had 228 yards to the pin and needed to carry it 215 yards. I went with the 2-iron and hit one of the shots of my life into that gorgeous hole; these days the youngsters are taking on the pin with as little as a 6- or 7-iron. It's a whole new ball game.

ing in your hands is matched perfectly to the dynamics of your swing. I'm a traditionalist through and through, but I have to confess to being totally hooked on testing out the latest models from my clubmaker, TaylorMade, and utilizing TrackMan swing and ball-flight analysis in a bid to get close to the numbers scientific research tells us produce the op-

timum distance. This is where the modern game is going. Nothing is a guess anymore. Whether it's in the field of biomechanics, the ballistics of club and ball technology, or the physics of swing path, angle of attack, spin, and ball flight, the science is out there to help you maximize your performance.

All you have to do is go out and embrace it.

SPEED, ANGLES, AND TRACKMAN NUMBERS...

IF WE WERE at the range hitting drivers, my initial advice to you would center on the *musts* that I focus on in my own swing. I would first remind you of the importance of the *knees* in establishing an athletic posture. From there, make a low and smooth first move away from the ball, before *completing* the shoulder turn for a solid backswing position. I want to see and feel my left shoulder fully turned under my chin as I stretch my torso to get loaded behind the ball. Once you achieve that, the *separation* at the start of the downswing is the bridge to unwinding your whole body in sync. Accelerating through the gears, I'd then stress

VIDEO LESSON:
TRACKMAN ANGLE OF ATTACK
To maximize the benefits of modern technology, you have to learn to strike the ball at the very bottom of the swing arc, just as the clubhead starts its ascent. With the benefit of TrackMan analysis, Nick Faldo explains the adjustments required.

again the importance of visualizing impact as a *passing-through* area—vital with a driver as you look to sweep the ball off the tee for the desired "rainbow" trajectory that optimizes carry and roll for distance.

So far, nothing new techniquewise. The emphasis is on making your swing fuller and better. The only way to increase distance is to increase your clubhead speed through the ball and to work on optimizing your launch angle with a pure strike. To do that, I would lean toward playing the ball forward in your stance so that you give yourself the best possible chance of "collecting" it just after the bottom of your swing arc—ideally "on the up." This is where I'd bring in TrackMan testing to identify the all-important numbers that are impossible to detect by simply watching ball flight. To maximize distance, you are looking for the most efficient impact possible with a high launch angle

and low spin—those are your twin goals. The quality of your ball-striking is wholly dependent on returning the clubface square to the ball on a natural path that is slightly inside-square-inside, so that you are able to deliver the true loft on the clubface. The modern tour player is looking for a launch angle of about 11 or 12 degrees (which ties in with the majority using a driver with between 9 and 10 degrees of loft) and a spin rate somewhere between 2,100 and 2,400 rpm. The beauty of using TrackMan's ingenious technology is that three or four shots is all it takes to generate a matrix of numbers that reveal the characteristics of your swing—that is, your clubhead speed, the angle of attack, the path (relative to your target line), and the backspin you generate. I have no doubt that this type of analysis will replace video as the most effective form of education. The numbers are absolute.

The only warning I need to give you here is that hitting balls with the benefit of this feedback is utterly addictive. I just wish I had had this technology when I started out. We use TrackMan at the Faldo Institute by Marriott (teaching facilities in Orlando and California), and I'm always intrigued to find out my own data and compare them to the current figures on the PGA Tour.

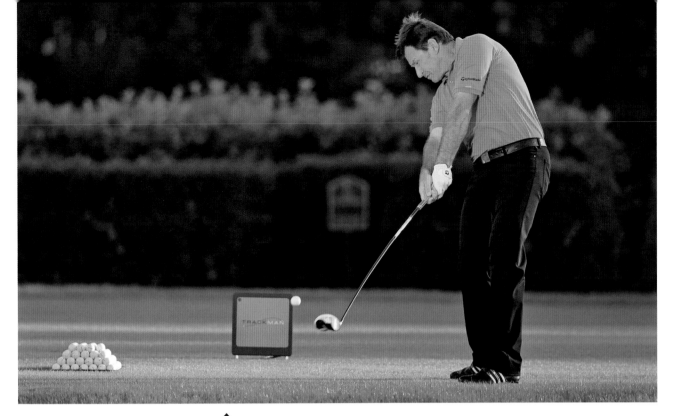

At my best these days, I generate clubhead speed in the range of 110 to 112 mph, and my angle of attack falls within the range of –1 degree to 0, giving me an average carry of 260 yards and a total distance of 275. In other words, I'm either striking fractionally down on the ball or catching it as the clubhead bottoms out at the lowest point in the arc. As much as I might try to catch the ball on the upswing (and I'm amazed how exaggerated a stance I have to make to see the slightest difference), it's actually quite difficult to achieve, although moving the ball significantly forward in the stance helps. One thing I've discovered quite recently is that I can increase my swing speed simply by lifting my left heel, keeping it

there in the backswing, and then super-clearing my hips on the way through. Raising that heel encourages a better rotation of the hips on the way back that benefits the swing generally, with the result that I achieve greater recoil speed on the way down (positively Tiger-*esque*!). A more reliable technique to employ on the course is breathing out through the swing, which I have found can add up to 3 mph to my clubhead speed!

INTERESTINGLY ENOUGH, figures from TrackMan revealed the following PGA Tour averages in 2011: clubhead speed of 112 mph, an angle of attack of –1 degree, a launch angle of 11 degrees, spin rate of 2,600 rpm, average carry of 269 yards, and total distance of 280. The ladies launch it higher, with

an average of +3 degrees upswing and 14-degree launch angle on the LPGA Tour in 2011. But there are one or two anomalies—and you won't be surprised to learn that the 2012 Masters champion, Bubba Watson, is one of them. I find this almost impossible to comprehend, but when Bubba hits that dinky cut-drive of his, his angle of attack is –5 degrees down; when he pegs it up super high to cut it loose at full throttle, he's 5 degrees on the up, and he creates clubhead speed in excess of 125 mph with a driver! That is just an incredible range of motion and delivery—and it proves Bubba is a unique player. Whether he's hitting a driver or a 9-iron, it's fascinating to watch the way he moves the ball forward or back in his stance to accommodate the shape of shot he's looking for. Remarkable—if unorthodox—artistry.

With the benefit of TrackMan analysis, clubfitters can match your swing to the type of equipment that delivers the desired launch—and there in a nutshell is modern clubfitting using technology to maximize your physical capability. The thing I love most about using this system is that I can translate these figures into images, thus making me more aware of what I'm actually doing with the club, which helps me determine what adjustment I need to make. So not only does this analysis enable you to match your equipment to your swing characteristics, but it gives you what amounts to an X-ray, providing a checklist of the key data personal to your swing—the angle of attack being one of the most significant. My attention is typically drawn to ways in which I can get the bottom of my swing arc *behind* the ball to achieve that desired launch angle. One of the most effective is to stay back on my right side for that split second as I change direction—that helps me to achieve the sensation of releasing the club on the up. I also like freeing my wrists so that I can release the clubhead as fully as possible.

Of course, the one danger with all of this technology is losing

A NUMBERS GAME: TrackMan analysis provides instant feedback on the key aspects of your swing, including clubhead speed and angle of attack—figures that can help you to pinpoint areas of improvement for optimum performance.

sight of the fundamentals that govern a solid swing. Technology can accomplish only so much. To drive the ball solidly, you need good technique—and it's all about forces working against one another as you coil and release, stretching out your muscles like strands of elastic, using resistance and recoil to generate speed. You need rhythm and timing. Watch the way a world-class player such as Adam Scott engineers the "sequencing" of his coiling motion. Study the ratio of the turn; it's that *sequencing* between knees, hips, belly, and shoulders that matters. The torque in a good swing starts from the ground up—that is, the knees rotate less than the hips, the hips less than the stomach, and the stomach less than the shoulders. This is what we mean by the gearing of your sequence,

and the quality of that body action relies on the quality of your footwork and the interaction you have with the ground.

With these fundamental swing dynamics on board, your goals should be to optimize your angle of attack and to rehearse golf-specific exercises to strengthen the key muscles that enable you to maintain good body angles more consistently. You may not have the time to train as hard as a tour pro, but if you can find 20 minutes three times a week, you'll notice a difference in your golf fitness. I do a lot of training in my address position, using a medicine ball and resistance bands. The body angles you create with your posture lie at the heart of your golf swing. The better you maintain them, the better the overall quality of your body motion will be—and the faster you'll be able to swing the club.

PAUSE FOR THOUGHT
THINK POSITION, PLAY THE PERCENTAGES

BEFORE WE GET carried away with idyllic visions of 300-yard drives, let me bring the conversation back to what I've always considered the key component of a good driving strategy: position in the fairway. Back in the early 1990s I had the pleasure of meeting Ben Hogan at his club, Shady Oaks, in Fort Worth, Texas, and he shared his thoughts on every aspect of the game. His no-nonsense philosophy on driving the ball still holds true, and it's one of the great lessons every golfer needs to learn (and one that's often overlooked in the relentless pursuit of length). For Hogan, the key to playing good golf was positioning your tee shot in a specific spot in the fairway. A drive was not measured purely in terms of yards, but analyzed in terms of position. If a hole featured a dogleg and the best look at the green was from the left side of the fairway, that was where he planned his shot to finish. Length off the tee was sometimes a factor but rarely his biggest concern. Like every great player, Hogan knew how and when to turn on the power. When you're faced with a long par 4 or a reachable par 5, the potential rewards might warrant the risk of turning up the heat. Otherwise it was much better to play for position and make certain of finding the short grass. These strands of common sense add up to a lesson in course management that should form the basis of your driving strategy.

THE DRIVER SWING

STRETCHING THE CONCEPT OF "COIL AND RELEASE"

TURNING OUR attention once again to the mechanics of a sound swing, one of the most significant lessons I learned over my career related to the concept of creating and maintaining *resistance* in the body. Like winding up a powerful spring, you use your body to build torque that is then released when you unwind. The speed you've wound up is then conducted and multiplied down through the arms and hands and into the clubhead. As we've discussed in some detail, the rotation of the body is the foundation of a sound golf swing. It is the engine that drives the motion. The more efficient you make it, the better it runs and the more reliably it performs.

With a driver in my hands, I've always liked to feel that I really *stretch* out the muscles in my upper body (in the torso and left shoulder), while my knees do all they can to resist the rotary motion of my trunk. That, for me, is the feeling of a good backswing. There was a time when I would have bracketed my hips with my lower body, but with the benefit of biomechanical study, we now know that allowing the hips to rotate a little more freely in the backswing enables them to recoil with greater speed in the downswing. That's how the young stars of today get their phenomenal speed. Writing in the original *A Swing for Life* in 1995, I suggested a ratio of 90-degree shoulder turn to 30-degree hip turn. These days I'm more inclined to advise allowing the hips the freedom to rotate through 35 to 40 degrees, depending on your flexibility, as long as you maintain flex in the right knee and thigh.

The reward for making a full turn in the backswing is that your first move back to the ball—often called the "power move"—is a largely instinctive chain reaction. My weight flows across to my left side almost before my arms have completed the backswing; throwing the gears into reverse activates the proper downswing sequence. In the backswing, my left shoulder pulls on my left hip and left knee, and that gets me fully turned and *loaded* away from the target. Once my weight has settled in the transition period, my left shoulder re-rotates back toward the target, which in turn pulls on the left hip. I've always loved that feeling: As my left side clears out of the way, I'm then free to release the whole right side of my body through the ball, pouring on the power with a committed release.

Once you've wound up your backswing, the timing of this transition determines the quality of the recoil and your speed through the ball. As you start to separate from the top, feel your left shoulder and left knee move together and pull away from that resisting right side. *Settle* into the downswing. Negotiate this subtle reactionary move, and you unlock the door to a downswing that explodes into the back of the ball. *Just remember that you*

must complete your backswing in order for that transition to be most effective. When you release the spring with this left-side separation, you automatically clear the way for your arms to fall into the slot as they accelerate the clubhead down into that channel approaching impact. The chain reaction is working 100 percent in your favor—as your weight flows across into your left side and your arms and club fall into the hitting position, your right shoulder, right hip, and right knee (in that order) can *fire* and add thrust as you rotate through the ball.

It is in precisely this area that the young, athletic players you see today are maximizing the dynamics of their motion to generate phenomenal speed through the ball. Pound for pound, 2011 U.S. Open champion Rory McIlroy is one of the longest hitters in the game. His speed comes from an explosion of his hips through the swing, and the figures will astonish you: In the blink of an eye, Rory's hips rotate from a position in excess of 40 degrees closed at the full extent of his backswing (that is, his hips turned away from the target) to around 60 degrees open at the moment the clubhead meets the ball. Figures such as these leave us in little doubt as to where speed and power originate.

The rotation of the body core creates a centrifugal force that accelerates the arms, hands, and clubhead. At each stage in the chain, the energy is multiplied—most spectacularly through the leverage in the shaft as the wrists finally snap through impact.

The message is loud and clear: If you want to increase your speed, you need to think about a more efficient, dynamic, and explosive motion with your body. The speed at which Rory is able to clear his hips in the downswing reminds me of Tiger's lightning-quick swing. Sadly, not all of us have that athletic ability (nor the "twitch factor" muscle speed that we see in so many young play-

ers today), but there are ways in which you can improve your rotation. As I mentioned earlier in this chapter, I've begun focusing more of my effort on the "core" rotation of the hips and abdomen, trying to turn a little further in the backswing and faster through the impact zone. My power source from my downswing is my left shoulder, and I'm better able to feel this when my hips turn freely in the backswing. Once through the transition, I then focus on pulling my left shoulder back down, clearing a strong left side through impact so my right arm can straighten and deliver the

power. Ben Hogan illustrated it perfectly when he said that he wished he had two right hands through impact. When you load and unwind correctly, you really can hit aggressively with your right side.

ANOTHER AREA OF focus for me was the elbows; I always liked the sensation of fast elbows through impact. If I can achieve that, my forearms and hands will be moving at an even greater speed, and I can whip the club through the ball. In my first instruction book, *The Faldo Formula,* I talked extensively about the "power whip" of the elbows through the impact

area, and it's a quality you see in all great ball-strikers. The best analogy I can give you is that it's a bit like whipping a towel with a whiplash action; you cannot generate your maximum speed unless your arms and elbows are "soft"—any hint of tension, and you deny yourself that burst of acceleration. So think about this when you practice with your driver. Play with "soft elbows" and go after the feeling of this "power whip" through the impact area. South Africa's Retief Goosen has always appeared to me to be a player who understands this implicitly, and he displays this

quality in what is a deceptively powerful swing. Retief accelerates the clubhead through the ball with incredible elbow and forearm speed—all working within the security of a rock-solid body action. Soft elbows facilitate this whiplash effect as the clubhead is released—a flash-speed of rotation, and *boom!*

So the clues are out there: To improve your distance off the tee, you must improve the dynamics of your golf swing. You have to wind and unwind the body more efficiently, and athletically. And you have to keep the muscles in your arms and hands relaxed so that you multiply and channel your speed effectively. This means doing everything we've discussed in the golf swing *that little bit better.* The better your body action, the more often you'll get the club into the right position, and the more you can enjoy swinging freely with the arms and hands. Those of you familiar with Hogan's *Modern Fundamentals of Golf* may remember those illustrations of Hogan with a motor inside his body and electrical wires running down his arms and to his hands—a terrific image. That is exactly how I want you to think about the way you generate speed in your swing. Use your body rotation to generate power, and let sparks fly as you freewheel the arms and the hands.

FULL SWING, GREATER "SET"

A WORD ON THE specific role of the wrists, and the timing of the full "set" in the backswing.

As I look at my swing over the years, one thing stands out: While I have rarely ever got the club-shaft to parallel in the backswing, I have at times been noticeably "short" at the top. Technically, the positions I was achieving were sound, but something was missing. I was conscious of being perhaps a little too "stiff" and inflexible at the top of my backswing, which inevitably cost me energy and speed in the recoil. Ultimately, the solution was simple: I strengthened my left-hand grip by about half an inch (that is, turning it clockwise on the club), and also worked on pinching my left thumb as "short" as comfortably possible on the grip. As a result of this adjustment, I found that I was able to achieve a much fuller and deeper *setting* of the club as I reached the top of the backswing (what we call "loading the shaft"). While my preference had always been to encourage a relatively early *setting* of the wrists with the irons, creating more width with the driver would see a more gradual setting all the way to the top of the backswing, the weight and momentum of the clubhead pulling on the wrists as I settled into the transition at the top of the swing—a subtle feature that adds to the dynamics of the recoil.#

TURN "DEEP" INTO RIGHT HIP AND THIGH

IF YOU WERE to poll the longest hitters in the world and ask each of them to nominate one thought for distance, I guarantee that most would say they try to swing *easier*. Jack Nicklaus always used to say that whenever he needed to cut loose a big drive, he actually felt like he made a slower move away from the ball. What he meant by that was he wanted to be sure he gave the muscles in his body the time to work properly, and wind up fully. This has always been my theory, too. With a driver in my hands, my thoughts turn to stretching out the bigger muscles in my upper body, and when I do this, I rely on my knees to do all they can to resist the rotary motion of my hips and trunk. That gets me fully coiled, or loaded. The first move back to the ball is then the vital go-between that ensures the continuity of

the chain reaction. The process works from the ground up—my weight flows across to my left side almost before my arms have completed the backswing, and throwing the gears into reverse activates the proper downswing sequence.

An interesting area of discussion concerns the role of the hips. In my era I worked on building a significant resistance in the lower body, which limited my hip turn to about 30 degrees. But you can overdo it, and the danger is that in trying to create that resistance, you actually stifle the natural rotation of the knees and hips. Interestingly

enough, during that meeting with Sam Snead I talked about in Chapter 4, he observed that I was prone to using too wide a stance, thus restricting my hip turn. My shoulders might make a full 90-degree turn, but my overall motion lacked *fluidity*, as my hips were not involved the way they should be. I made use of Mr. Snead's advice and narrowed my stance a little to free up my hip rotation. The outcome was that my upper body could turn more freely, adding a valuable beat to the timing of my backswing coil. As a result, I was able to achieve a much better recoil through

impact and my arms were able to swing more effectively, all of which put me back in touch with my natural rhythm.

In between hitting drivers on the range I make a point of regularly hitting a few iron shots with my feet close together, just to keep in tune with that rotation. I also rehearse this backswing exercise: I keep my eyes closed to heighten the sensation of turning *deep* into the right hip, getting my left shoulder under the chin, and turning my back on the target—all while *posting* against that flexed right knee and thigh.#

DRILL

LEARN TO FREEWHEEL YOUR RIGHT SIDE

O**NE OF MY** favorite warm-up drills is swinging with my right arm only, with my focus on turning and coiling my upper body against a flexed and braced right knee. This is all about experiencing the sensation of those forces working against one another. Take a driver in your right hand and try this before the next time you play. Make a slow-motion swing with just your right hand on the club and feel every muscle in your body as you stretch and coil your way to the top of the backswing. Let your right hip rotate behind you to get you into that *loaded* position. Hold it there. Close your eyes and ingrain the feeling of this stretch.

Another motion that has the same effect is turning your left shoulder across to a position above your right knee. This really gets your upper body stretched behind the ball, but only if you keep that right knee and right thigh braced. Can you feel the big muscles in your torso stretch as you reach the top of your backswing? Hold it for a few seconds and then release the right arm as hard as you can through impact all the way to a wraparound finish. Get your right side firing, and finish with your right shoulder low, pointing left of the target. With a driver in your hands, there's no better swing thought than that.#

DRILL

SHALLOW YOUR ATTACK FOR A CLEAN SWEEP

AS I IMPROVED my body action in the mid-1980s, one of the by-products was a more rounded, shallow swing into the back of the ball. By lowering the plane of my swing relative to that of the backswing (the natural consequence of winding and unwinding my body correctly), I was able to deliver clubhead speed more efficiently through impact. This is something I've been reminded of using TrackMan analysis. The science tells us that angle of attack is the key to distance. You achieve ideal launch with your driver when the bottom of your swing arc is three or four inches ahead of the club meeting the ball, so that you are actually striking it in the early stages of *ascent*. One way to test and develop your skill in this area is to hit balls off a high tee using your 3-wood. Play the ball up in your stance, opposite the inside of the left heel; settle

THE BETTER your rotation, the more you are able to shallow the delivery of the clubhead for more solid ball-striking, greater speed, and greater distance.

your weight just slightly in favor of your right side; and work on freewheeling through the ball with a shallow delivery that catches the ball flush. *Collect* the ball off the peg, don't *hit* at it. Do this drill for a few minutes to build confidence at the bottom of your swing arc, then develop the same feel with the driver.

Another exercise I recommend to groove a shallow and more powerful attack involves finding a slope that allows you to spend a few minutes hitting shots with the ball positioned a few inches above the level of your feet (also a go-to exercise

that will help slicers get their swing path back into neutral). Use a middle iron and get used to the sensation of turning your body correctly to swing in sympathy with the slope. This is a great exercise for anyone who tends to get a little steep on the ball. In just a few minutes your swing will feel nicely rounded and compact as you adjust it to compensate for the fact that the ball is slightly above the level of your stance, and your shoulders will be encouraged to turn back and through on a relatively level plane. As you hold your finish, the ball will fly with right-to-left spin.#

PAUSE FOR THOUGHT

NERVOUS? SPEED UP YOUR STOMACH

UNDER ANY SORT of pressure, there's often a tendency to *quit* on your body action: The hips and stomach decelerate in the moments before impact; there's no confidence and no commitment to the shot. This is one reason so many amateurs leave the ball out to the right of their target. As the turning motion effectively comes to a halt, the ball flies exactly where their chest is facing at the conclusion of the swing. So any time you feel a little nervous, or you begin to leak shots right, turn your attention to the rotation of your stomach and commit to turning your belly all the way through the shot. One of the most effective ways to feel this body action is to hold a driver out at waist height and swish the clubhead like you're hitting a baseball. Feel your shoulders turn fully back and through. The faster the stomach moves, the greater the acceleration of the clubhead, and the louder the swish. Repeat this several times and then try to re-create that sound with your regular swing. The beauty of this quick and simple exercise is that it teaches you the discipline of building acceleration gradually, one of the keys to maximizing clubhead speed for impact.

DRILL

FOCUS ON YOUR LEG ACTION— AND CONTAIN YOUR POWER FROM THE GROUND UP

D**RIVE THE LEGS,"** I was told as a young player. Of course, in the 1970s this was all the rage, an aggressive leg action regarded as a source of power. But the trouble with driving your legs is that as a consequence of your lower body moving vigorously toward the target, your upper body can get left behind. You end up *trapped*, with nowhere for your arms to go. Your upper and lower body have no working relationship, so you either block the shot to the right or *flip* at it with your hands, hoping there's a chance you'll recover—but you live in fear of the left side of the golf course. Neither is a reliable way to play the game.

One of the fundamental lessons throughout this book has focused on the stabilizing role of the legs, and with the driver this is more important than ever to balance and support the rotary motion of the torso. Quite simply, the more athletic your leg action, the more it will enhance the winding and unwinding of your upper body—and the better the dynamics of your body action, the more recoil speed you will enjoy as you unwind through the hitting area. If you are prone to driving a little too hard with your lower body, try hitting a few shots with your toes curled up inside your shoes; this will quiet even the most exaggerated leg action.

Study the left leg here as I work through the transition; it returns to "post" the resistance in the downswing, but does not buckle to the outside of the left foot. That's a distinction you must be aware of. A solid leg action *contains* this transition, whereupon the right side of the body is free to explode through the ball.#

DRILL

MUCH TO GAIN FROM A DOWNHILL LIE . . .

IF YOU HAVE trouble feeling or picturing a "posted" left leg, go out and hit a few balls off a steep downhill slope. I used to love doing this, as there are so many benefits that come your way. As you take your stance with an 8-iron, try to stay centered even though your feet and knees are set at different levels. You will experience a raft of new sensations as you hit a few gentle shots, specifically in the way your left leg straightens and holds/supports the unwinding of your body through the ball. Other benefits of this drill include:

1. The downhill lie will prevent you from taking the club back too much inside—it eliminates any tendency to roll the forearms into the backswing.
2. It teaches you to hold off the club through the ball with a late release. (If you cast the club—i.e., throw the right shoulder forward and release the wrists too early on the way down—you are likely to hit the ground before the ball.)
3. You really do have to stretch your right side down the slope to *collect* the ball, which is great for the quality of your striking.
4. You will be made aware of the importance of balance and strength in the legs.

The key to a sound, repeating technique is to use the pressure you apply into the ground to control the sequence of your swing. In the backswing, use the right knee and thigh as a *post* to load and coil around; just as important, it then remains stable momentarily as you ease into the transition so that you have something to pull away from. Wind it up, wait for it, and then give it some speed on the way through. In the whole scheme of things, the transition involves a tiny series of movements, but the timing of each element is vital. Make a swing in slow motion to feel and appreciate the ground force through the balls of your feet, and then release the right knee to *kiss* the left knee at the finish. That will get you rotating all the way through to the left side and ensure a straight-line finish, with the body aiming left of the target. Remember: When the body is working well, you can put your emphasis on your forearms and your core, which is a powerful combination. #

FOCUS ON THE NO. 1 SPOT . . .

I'VE NEVER STOOD over a ball and visualized a dead-straight drive. That doesn't exist in my mind. We all have a favorite shape of shot, and mine has always been a gentle fade. One of the best driving tips I ever had came from my first coach, Ian Connelly, at Welwyn Garden City, where I learned to play the game as a junior. Ian called it "hitting the No. 1 spot," and it was a simple focusing exercise that involved placing my concentration one or two dimples inside the middle line as I looked down on the ball. This was "the No. 1 Spot," and that was my target as I set up with all my long clubs. If I could return the clubface on that exact spot, I had no fear of the ball ever going left—my swing would be meeting the ball fractionally from the inside, a couple of dimples toward me. That produced a very slight fade off the tee, my stock shot over my 30 years on tour. Many golfers these days put a dot on their ball or mark a line with a Sharpie pen, and doing this enables you to practice this simple exercise every time you tee up. Place the ball on the tee so that dot or line is just inside the target line as you look at it standing behind the ball and surveying the shot, and then visualize your swing coming inside to nail that No. 1 Spot perfectly every time. This is all about returning the straight face of your driver to the radius of the ball to create that subtle spin. Try it next time you practice—it could give you a shot you can trust under pressure.#

VIDEO LESSON: TRACKMAN "OVER THE TOP"
The dreaded "over-the-top" fault costs you speed and distance—the bane of slicers the world over! Here, Nick Faldo shows you a couple of quick fixes that will get your swing back on the desired inside track.

TURNING ON THE POWER
MY KEY THOUGHTS

BEFORE WE LOOK at a driver sequence in detail and pull out the main power points, let me deal with a couple of specific aspects of the setup position that a lot of amateur golfers fail to recognize as being significant to the outcome of a shot.

The first is how high you should tee the ball. A lot depends on circumstance. For a regular drive, I would tee up the ball with at least half of it visible above the top edge of the club. This ties in with the powerful upward sweep of the ball we are looking for through impact. The modern driver, with its oversize head and deep face, requires you to tee it up invitingly. Downwind, I might tee the ball a little more generously to achieve a higher ball flight. If I'm hitting into the wind, then it'd be fractionally lower—but don't go too low, or you'll hit down and create too much sidespin. The modern ball is good for sailing through the wind, so you really don't need to tee it as low as we used to for a lower flight—you're simply aiming to generate the minimum backspin with a shallow angle of attack.

As for the ball position within the stance, you should experiment with this to achieve your optimum launch angle. Playing the ball forward in my stance, opposite my left toe, is one of the significant changes I've made in recent years. To maximize the performance of modern technology, you're looking to catch the ball on the *up,* and playing the ball forward is now a standard feature of the setup position with a driver. I vary the ball position two or three inches between the inside of my left heel and the toe of my left foot. That might not sound like a lot, but it's enough to affect ball flight. You need to check this detail regularly. A lot of amateurs tell me they play the ball inside the left heel, when it's actually nearer the middle of the stance, which often explains a severely downward angle of attack.

Tee height and ball position are really the key variables you can experiment with, so go out and see what you can achieve with different combinations. I would advise against setting too much of your weight on your right foot (for the right-handed player), as I believe you make a more neutral swing with your weight evenly split, encouraging weight shift in the swing itself rather than presetting it on the right foot, leaning away from the target and placing the right shoulder too low relative to the left. I don't like to see a manufactured slant across the shoulders; it's much better to keep them natural.

A question I'm often asked is "What's the difference between a driver swing and a regular iron swing?" By now you should have a good idea of our goals—we're not looking to do very much different with the swing itself, but the angle of attack has to be optimized for distance. On iron shots, you're looking for the slightly downward strike that takes ball, then divot. With a driver, you want to sweep the ball off the tee, and minor adjustments in your setup position reflect that intention. Then it's business as usual. When I practice, I try not to hit too many drives in succession. I keep a wedge handy, throttle back, and alternate by hitting a few pitch shots in between. That helps me maintain my feel and rhythm, and keeps my timing sharp. (It also helps you maintain that natural swing plane, as we discussed in earlier chapters.) If there's a surefire way of losing your tempo, it is firing on all cylinders too hard and for too long. Don't get fixated on hitting your driver.

THE SETUP
A SOLID BASE FOR A SOLID SWING

FOR OPTIMUM balance and mobility, I set up with the insides of my feet spread to approximately shoulder width. My knees flexed, I settle my weight perhaps 55:45 in favor of the right side, but I don't accentuate the shoulder angle any more than normal. I find that I create just the right tilt in my body angle when I get my right butt cheek slightly down relative to the left. My arms hang comfortably, and my hands are just slightly behind the ball, which is teed forward in my stance. I waggle the clubhead a couple of times to keep my forearms and hands loose, and gently bounce on the knees to pep up my legs. I want my muscles to work like strong strands of elastic. You won't hit the ball a long way if you're tight and tense (remember those "soft" elbows!). Everything must be ready to *flow*.

THE TAKEAWAY
THINK *LOW AND SMOOTH* FOR WIDTH

WHEN I'M HITTING it well off the tee, I'm focused on getting my upper body behind the ball in the backswing with a good windup, and the takeaway holds the key. The trigger I use is *low and smooth*. I concentrate on turning my shoulders, my arms, and the club away from the ball in one piece, which promotes a wide arc. At the same time, I sense that my weight begins to flow across to the right side, and so the coiling process is under way. The *sequencing* in the swing starts here, as does the setting of the wrists.

HALFWAY BACK
PROGRESSIVELY *LOADING* THE WRISTS

THE *SEQUENCING* OF my body turn is now well into gear as I rotate and coil over the stability of my feet and knees. I am aware of the sensation of my left arm swinging across my chest, and my wrists are now really starting to *load* as the club swings up. The gearing effect is now evident as my shoulders have rotated slightly more than my hips, my hips slightly more than my knees—and the dynamics of this motion are maximized as my shoulders *complete* the backswing turn, stretching the muscles in the torso and carrying the club all the way to a sound position at the top.

TO THE TOP
LOADING THE SPRING

TURNING YOUR UPPER body against a flexed right knee is one of my *musts* for building a powerfully coiled backswing. The spring is now fully loaded; you can almost feel the energy bursting out. I have a great sense of stretch-ing my chest as I turn my left shoulder under my chin, while keeping that right knee and thigh *posted*. My wrists set progressively through the backswing, the full and final setting occurring as the momentum of the clubhead pulls on the wrists at the very top of the swing. This compact swinging of the arms, combined with a full body turn, is a solid combina-tion. I don't like to see the shaft get too far past horizontal at the top. There's a slight cupping in the back of my left hand, and my left thumb is supporting the shaft. Here, it's under control.

THE POWER MOVE
UNWIND IN SYNC

IN ALL MY years studying the golf swing, one of the most sound conclusions I've made is that every great player starts his downswing with a subtle reflexive action in his lower body—usually the left foot or knee. My own feeling is that my left knee and left shoulder move together, a coordinated move that signals the shift toward the target. In that split second, my body is actually moving in two directions at once. My wrists, you will notice, have remained fully hinged—ready to crack the whip through the impact area.

IMPACT
ROTATE LEFT AND COLLECT THE BALL

WHEN MY BODY action is ticking over nicely, I enjoy a great sense of freedom as I rotate through the shot. Remember, this is a *passing-through area*—a moment in a flowing, continuous motion. My body is the engine generating the power while my arms and hands transmit that energy down through the shaft to the ball. Looking for that optimal launch angle, I have a sense of staying behind the ball for as long as possible before my right shoulder, right hip, and right knee *fire* and add thrust through impact, where speed obviously matters the most. When I practice, I often say to myself "left side clears, right side drives." On a good day I feel that I punish the back of the ball with the right shoulder as it rotates under my chin.

THE FINISH

TURN *THROUGH* THE BALL

THERE'S A wonderful feeling of being pulled by the momentum of the clubhead as you unwind to a full and balanced finish. Everything about the body language you display here should reflect the fact that you have released the clubhead at speed and with absolute commitment through the ball—which is a *must* with the driver.

Throughout the book I have stressed the importance of the follow-through and the fact that understanding where you want to finish your swing can positively assist you in getting there. That's certainly the case here. The key is that you actually finish your swing with your chest and belt buckle facing *left* of the target line—evidence that you have recoiled all the way through the ball. In the final analysis, most of my weight is supported on the left side, my spine vertical, hands low behind my neck. It's a natural conclusion to a freewheeling through-swing—and a position I can hold in balance for several seconds. That's actually a great test of the stability at the heart of your swing: Can you hold the pose until you see the ball land?

1989 *The Masters, Augusta, Georgia*

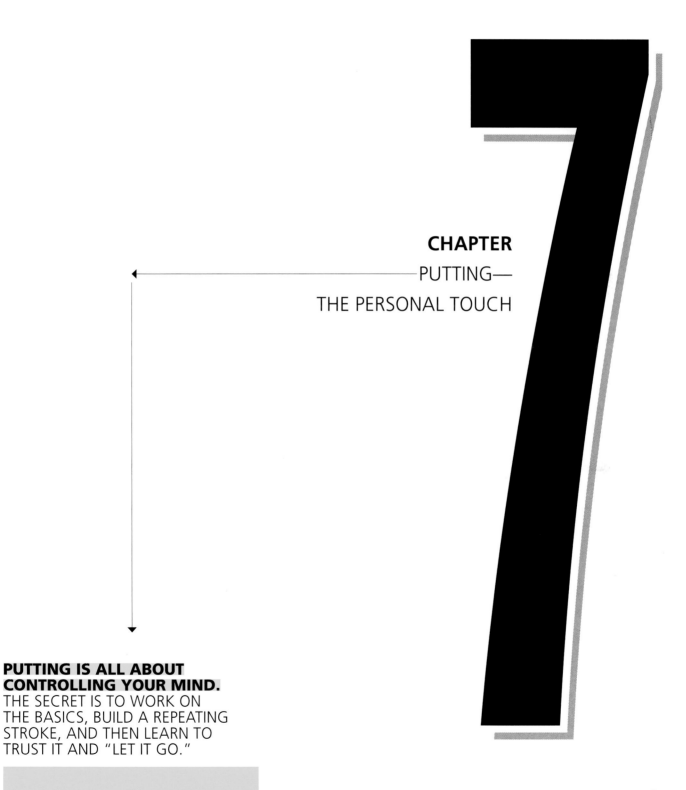

CHAPTER

PUTTING—
THE PERSONAL TOUCH

**PUTTING IS ALL ABOUT
CONTROLLING YOUR MIND.**
THE SECRET IS TO WORK ON
THE BASICS, BUILD A REPEATING
STROKE, AND THEN LEARN TO
TRUST IT AND "LET IT GO."

LOOK AROUND the practice green at any professional tournament and you will soon appreciate the fact that putting is a very personal affair. No other aspect of the game is as open to individual interpretation . . . and in the never-ending search for the perfect stroke—or at least one that will get them through 18 holes—golfers have tried just about every grip configuration imaginable."

These are the opening lines to the putting section of my original *A Swing for Life*. I couldn't have imagined back then, 17 years ago, just how prophetic my words would be. About the most radical piece of advice in that chapter was the suggestion that a left-hand-low grip might be worth a try, to get a feeling for pulling the putter through the ball, and releasing the stroke on line—these days, as we have all seen, almost anything goes.

As someone who values golf's traditions, I have to say I'm not entirely comfortable with the belly- and broom-handle putters that are now such a feature of the modern game. In my mind, the skill and the challenge lie in creating a golf *swing,* not a "hinge." I don't agree with it. When you anchor the top of the grip against your chest, the putterhead traces a natural path, like opening and closing a door. It's an automatic stroke, hinged against the body. To me, that's not golf. But having explored the technique involved at putting research facilities with my club suppliers, TaylorMade— and while the Rules of Golf allow these techniques of stroke—I am not at all surprised to see more and more players turning to them, and especially the belly models.

Not so long ago, the long putter was seen as the last resort for players whose nerves had taken over. Not anymore. That stigma is gone. The reason players are using them today is that the technology proves this is the way to repeat a reliable putting stroke, rolling the ball more consistently, holing more putts.

If you're serious about exploring every avenue in the pursuit of playing better golf, I urge you to go to a putting lab and have your technique analyzed. I'm fascinated by today's technology and regularly visit TaylorMade for a tune-up. I hit a few putts with different putters—my traditional method plus the belly being favorites for comparison—and analysis of each of my strokes pops up on the computer. Not only does the feedback tell me which stroke is the most effective for repeating a solid on-line strike on the ball, but the technicians have the skill and experience to suggest adjustments to correct faults that may have crept in (at least 99 percent of them have to do with alignment) to make my natural stroke better. It may be something as simple as adding half an inch to the shaft or adjusting the lie by a degree. These slight adjustments alone are worth the price of admission.

THE BOTTOM LINE is that all guesswork has been taken out of the game. In the same way TrackMan offers you a virtual X-ray of your golf swing, the technology used in putting analysis reveals, in black and white, what you have to do

WEBB SIMPSON **is one of the finest exponents of the belly putter, and his U.S. Open victory at Olympic Club will doubtless inspire more youngsters to experiment with this style.**

to make a better stroke. Whether you use a conventional putter or prefer a long one, every single detail of your putting technique can be quickly and easily fine-tuned, so when you do head out to the putting green, you are not searching for a stroke—you know with absolute certainty that you have nailed the fundamentals and are aiming the putter correctly, starting the ball on your chosen line and producing a pure roll.

Of course, the fact that we're even talking about so many options only serves to highlight the importance of the "game within a game" when it comes to your ability to score. Nothing is more soul-destroying than striking the ball well but then wasting golden opportunities on the green. To achieve any sort of success in amateur golf, which I define as achieving low single figures, I'd say you have to be looking at a putting average of 30 putts per round or below. On tour you need to shave another three or four off that to be anywhere near the leaders.

THE SETUP

BUILD CONSISTENCY FROM THE GROUND UP

IN THE FULL swing, we used that club on the ground to confirm all matters of alignment in the process of building a good posture. When it comes to putting, the best piece of advice I can give—and it will cost you no more than a few bucks from your local hardware store—is to invest in a builder's chalk line. Find a straight putt, draw out a line of chalk, and you have a ready-made practice station. Whether they use a conventional or a long putter, this is about as complicated

as most tour players like to make it on the practice green. A chalk line provides the perfect assist in building good setup habits and specifically helping you to position your body lines square to the target line in preparation to roll the ball into the center of the cup. We're talking *instant feedback*. The moment you stand over the ball, you're aware of the line running directly into the middle of

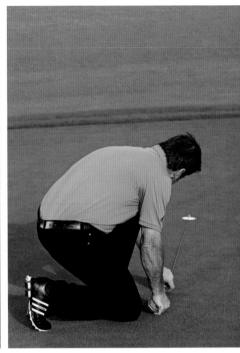

the hole, and you know that it is a dead straight putt, which is great for your confidence. It's then a case of repetition, going through the motions, and holing putt after putt.

So with that chalk line just visible on the green, let me talk you through the way I see a solid stroke taking shape.

First, we'll look at your posture. Study the best players in the world, and you'll see that all reliable putting strokes revolve around a consistent spine and shoulder angle. You don't see too many top players who lean excessively forward, or who stand with their weight too far back on their heels. Just as we established in the full swing, you need "dynamic balance." Your body is relaxed, but at the same time solid. The pendulum-style method I have always trusted is controlled predominantly by the bigger muscles in the shoulders, and by its very nature demands a fairly orthodox setup position in relation to that line. To give my arms and shoulders the freedom they need to work and interact correctly, I flex my knees, stick my rear end out, and bend from the hips until my arms hang naturally in front of my body. Free of tension, the two elbows list in toward my chest, and when I bring the palms of my hands together on the grip, the putter becomes merely an extension of my arms.

A BUILDER'S **chalk line is invaluable not only as a source of reference that enables you to cement sound fundamentals of alignment in a consistent setup routine, but also as a tool with which to monitor the path of your stroke as you hit putts.**

VIDEO LESSON:
PUTTING—A GENERAL
OVERVIEW
The fundamentals of posture, alignment, and ball position are as important in putting as they are in the full swing. Nick Faldo shares his thoughts on a putting style that has stood the test of time.

Recognize a pattern here? The technique we're looking to build is similar to the full swing in that you want to create a sound structure with your body. It enables you to control the swinging of the arms, hands, and putter with the movement of the torso. *Feel within a framework.* A good setup is designed to allow you to make a consistent stroke through the ball and get it rolling on your chosen line to the hole. Just about everywhere else in the game I would advise you to experiment with ball position within your stance, but there's a consensus of

opinion in putting: The ideal strike is one where the putter meets the ball as it travels level with the ground or in the very early stages of ascent, so it catches the ball on the equator and sets it rolling "end-over-end." It's certainly not a coincidence that most good putters play the ball forward, somewhere between the middle of their stance and inside their left heel. A consistent ball position is another of my *musts,* and you should check this feature of your

setup regularly. To do this, take your normal posture, then drop a ball from your left eye, and mark where it lands. Play from within an inch or so of that point, and you will find that you are able to strike up on the ball freely through impact.

Your perception of what "straight" looks like depends on the relationship you have with the ball position. In other words, it's all down to your eye-line and posture. Most of us see a straight line with our eyes either directly over the ball or fractionally inside the ball-to-target line. It's extremely

rare for a player to see a straight line with his eye-line outside the ball. Clearly, any imbalance between your perception and reality will lead to compensations in your stroke, and a thorough investigation of your alignment preferences is part and parcel of a consultation with a good putting technician. To me, this is another *must*. After checking all of your key details, you'll be able to identify any adjustments that need to be made to your putter, in terms of length and lie angle, to help you establish a good, consistent posture. In the context of the game,

ONCE YOU'VE established good posture and square alignment, the stroke itself is governed by the shoulders—with the arms, hands, and putter moving smoothly in response to create a smooth pass through the ball.

it's a small price to pay for what amounts to your ability to shoot lower and lower scores.

With your putter "fitted" to suit you and a clear perception of the line all the way into the hole, working on the basics of a good putting motion with the security of that chalk line on the green

makes a lasting impression. It's the best exercise you can possibly do. As a source of reference, it confirms the alignment of your feet, hips, shoulders, and eyes all parallel to the target line, a natural position from which to make a pure pendulum stroke. Make this a regular feature of your practice routine, and you'll prevent basic errors from creeping in.

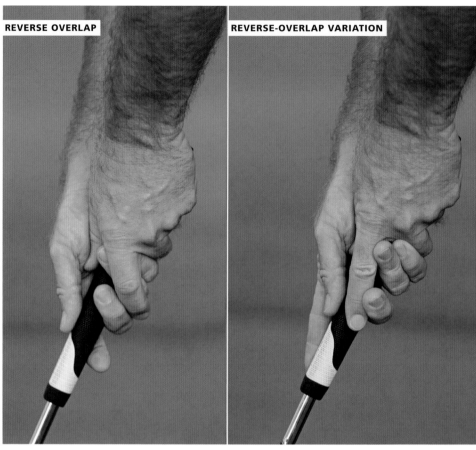

REVERSE OVERLAP

REVERSE-OVERLAP VARIATION

THE STANDARD REVERSE-OVERLAP GRIP is the most popular on tour for the way it enables the two hands to work as one secure guiding unit while retaining a high degree of feel. You should experiment with this and the many alternatives until you find a grip that is both comfortable and functional.

FIND THE GRIP THAT GIVES *YOU* THE BEST SOURCE OF FEEL AND CONTROL

GIVEN THE TRENDS on tour these days, we could soon see the first instruction book devoted entirely to the multitude of ways in which you can—and indeed should—experiment with the positioning of your hands on the grip. Over the years, I experimented with various different styles, and always regarded having the palms opposing each other as a "standard"—a convention that

has been knocked sideways with the arrival of the saw, the piccolo, and the pencil grips, and whatever other configurations pop up on tour before you read this book. But let me share my thoughts on the regular styles I've trusted, along with a look at some of the more exotic variations.

For most of my career I used what is known as the "reverse-overlap," in which the hands join together comfortably, neither one overriding the other. I tend to regard the left as the guiding hand, while the right is very much responsible for feeling the pace of the putt. This is reflected in the way I hold the club, as illustrated here. The grip runs diagonally through the palm of my left hand and is secured with pressure applied mainly by the

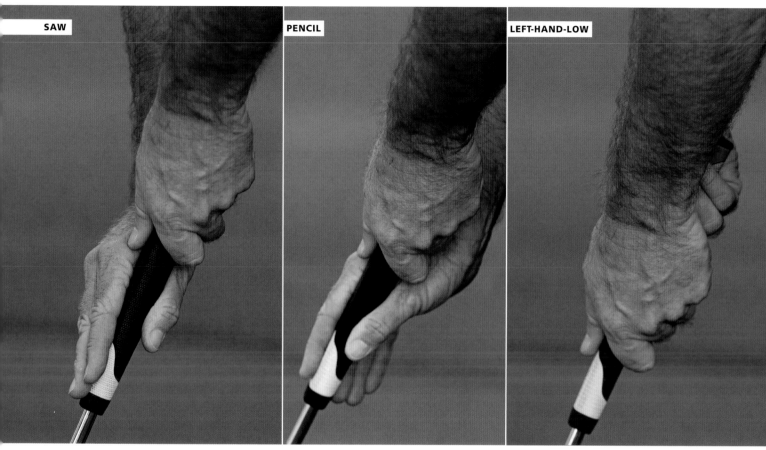

SAW

PENCIL

LEFT-HAND-LOW

A MODERN TREND has seen more exotic grips emerge, both the saw and the pencil styles featuring a secure left-hand position at the top of the grip and the diminished role of the right hand as it caresses the grip primarily in the fingers.

THE LEFT-HAND-LOW GRIP promotes a more natural pendulum-style stroke controlled by the shoulders, making it one of the most popular alternatives among tour players.

last three fingers. That's a firm, not a tight, hold, and the grip is held a little higher in the palm of the hand than for a regular swing, which helps to diminish wrist action. That aligns the shaft with my forearms, which adds to the symmetry of the stroke. Using an orthodox hold, I sense that my left hand has control of the putter, but

at the same time the muscles in my wrist and forearm are relaxed.

The right hand caresses the club more in the fingers. And just as I look for in the full swing, the "trigger" unit that is formed between the right thumb and forefinger makes for a sensitive component—that's something you should foster. To enrich your sense of feel, make sure

the thumbs rest lightly on top of the shaft. Treat those as your sensor pads.

As far as the details go, it's up to you to find a method of joining and placing the fingers that both is comfortable and allows you to maintain a consistent pressure in the forearms. That's important. You will find you putt better when

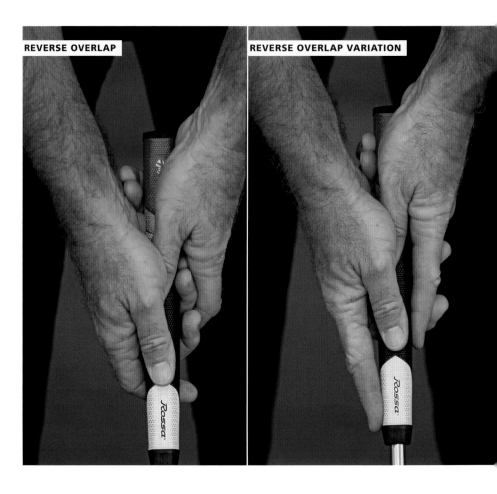

REVERSE OVERLAP

REVERSE OVERLAP VARIATION

the muscles in your forearms are relaxed, so your hands and arms are able to feel the weight and momentum of the putterhead as you swing it back and forth. Among tour players who use the regular style grip, the most popular is the reverse-overlap, which earned the name for the way the left forefinger is draped across the fingers of the right hand. Not only does this feel snug, but that extra support enables your two hands to work as one guiding unit.

As for the alternatives that I've used in my career, I always liked the way the left-hand-low made finding a comfortable setup position that much easier. Not only does placing the left hand below the right help to level the shoulders, but the arms and the elbows are encouraged to fall nicely in toward the body, forming more of a true pendulum, with the

shoulders in control of the motion. The right elbow, particularly, is placed comfortably toward the side of your body, where it remains throughout the stroke. I always enjoyed the great feeling of my left arm and the shaft working together back and through, the putterhead traveling on a shallow arc and giving me a solid, consistent strike on the back of the ball. With the sensation of pulling the putterhead with the back of my left hand, the face is square all the

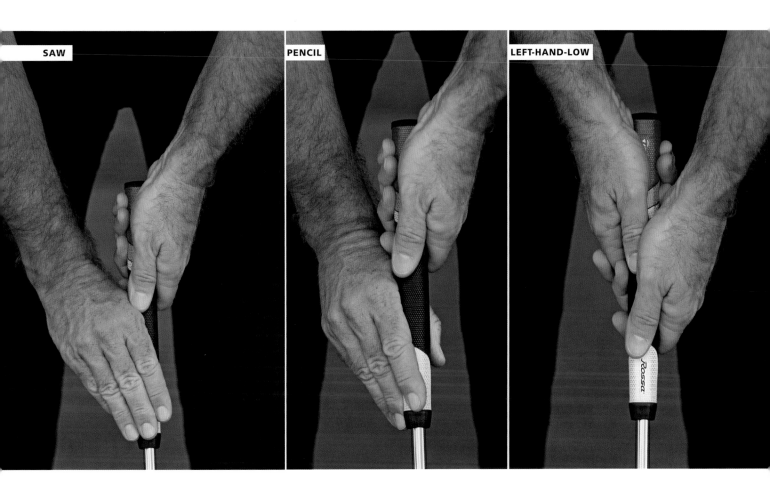

SAW   **PENCIL**   **LEFT-HAND-LOW**

way through impact; the stroke is on line for longer. Interestingly enough, Jack Nicklaus always said that if he started his career today, he would adopt the left-hand-low putting stroke, which should be reason enough for you to try it.

The variations that have become popular recently—notably the saw and pencil styles—all feature a solid left-hand position

securing the club high in the palm of the left hand. The difference in style is then all about the way in which the right hand is applied, as you see here in the accompanying photographs. Sergio Garcia has seen success recently using the pencil-type grip, and he putts well with it, particularly on fast greens. Watching him, it seems that the key to using this sort of stroke is to aim the putterface conventionally, using both hands, and then carefully adjust the position of the

right hand at the final moment. The momentum of the stroke still emanates from the shoulders, the fingers of the right hand resting lightly on the grip and adding only a gentle acceleration through the ball. Essentially, the left hand maintains control of the putter while the upper body governs the overall motion.

DRILL

DEVELOP FEEL AND FLOW WITH THE RIGHT HAND ONLY

WHEN I WORK on the mechanics of my stroke, I think in terms of the role each part of my body plays. Again, as with the full swing, I'm looking for a chain reaction. The shoulders control the motion—they create momentum as they rotate gently back and forth. This is why when you work on your stroke, you need to always make sure your alignment is square to that chalk line, according to the natural way of things.

I don't agree that the hands and wrists should be eliminated from the equation. If you isolate the hands, you end up with a fairly wooden stroke, with little to no feel. To create the flow and momentum that we see in a good, accelerating motion, you need the hands and wrists to be "alive," free to flex and respond naturally. All the best putters have this "lag" in their stroke. They nurture this freedom in the wrists and forearms, which enables them to produce controlled acceleration with a relatively small stroke.

To appreciate this sensation, try hitting putts with just your right hand on the grip (the left hand if you're a left-handed player). The weight of the putterhead will act upon your wrist, and you won't be able to resist that subtle feeling as you change direction. The overall control for the movement of your right hand and forearm comes from the shoulders, but you *feel* the putterhead in the right hand. I usually place my left hand on the right bicep to steady my upper right arm and shoulder unit, which emphasizes the control that comes from this area. Use this drill to get a positive feeling of flow and release, and then go after that same feeling with both hands on the putter.#

FIRM LEFT WRIST
PULLS THE PUTTERFACE
THROUGH

ONE OF THE most destructive faults in putting is the left wrist collapsing through impact, and again this is something the

reverse-handed grip can help eliminate. Placing the left hand below the right makes you aware of the rock-solid position of the left hand and wrist through the stroke. I always enjoyed keeping my head still until the ball was out of my peripheral vision. For anyone with even the slightest flutter in the hands through impact, the left-hand-low grip is a serious option worth trying. Placing the left hand below the right gets the shoulders level and certainly helps you to make a natural backswing, keeping the putter low and the face square to the path. The sense of pulling the left hand through the ball can be easier to repeat than releasing the right hand, and whether or not you choose to try the left-hand-low style, rehearsing your stroke with just your left hand on the grip is a great way to appreciate the positive feeling that you are looking for.#

ROCK THE SHOULDERS TO CREATE MOMENTUM

H**ERE'S A POPULAR DRILL** that will help you develop a good sense of the way the upper arms, chest, and shoulders work together in a repeating pendulum-type stroke. After setting up in your putting posture, trap a club (or an umbrella) across your chest, just above your elbows, and keep it there as you bring your arms into their final position and place the putterhead behind the ball. Immediately you get a heightened sensation of the relationship between the arms and shoulders. Then, keeping the club (or umbrella) in place, work on rocking your right shoulder around and down to move the putterhead back and through. Feel the coordinated mechanism of shoulders, arms, hands, and club working as one unit. If you keep your head still and your motion oiled with a good rhythm, you should soon be enjoying a repeating stroke as that connection between arms, shoulders, and body controls the movement of the putter.#

VIDEO LESSON: PUTTING DRILL
Nick Faldo demonstrates a tour-proven exercise that will enable you to experience the sensation of a shoulder-controlled pendulum-style putting stroke.

HOLING OUT

KEEP YOUR PUTTER ON THE RAIL

TOUR PLAYERS SPEND more time working on the 5- to 10-foot range than almost anything else—these are the putts that define a round of golf. Hole a high percentage, and your score tumbles into the red; miss more than you make, and you're treading water. Nothing in this game is more frustrating than failing to convert the good shots you've hit to set up these opportunities. So commit yourself to working on these "money putts," fine-tuning the essential mechanics of your stroke with that chalk line as your constant companion.

As you settle over the ball, take a lot of confidence from the fact that your key body lines—hips, shoulders, eyes, and forearms—are perfectly in tune with that chalk line. The more often you practice like this, the more you'll cement the sensations of being "square" and the more you'll trust the technique on the course. Hit a few balls, and learn from the feedback. Make sure the putterface remains square to the path of your stroke. There should be no dramatic twisting or turning, although a number of great putters have adapted a personal style. Tom Watson used a technique that saw the putterface travel slightly shut on the way back to square at impact and down the line to the hole. Seve Ballesteros had a tendency to work the putter square to fractionally open. In the late 1980s, I went through a period in which I believed in keeping the putterhead low on the way back and then swinging it "up" through the ball, and would adjust my posture with a high left shoulder and low right to make this style work. (To my mind, Phil Mickelson has that look on the greens; in his case, being left-handed, he keeps his right shoulder high and left side low to encourage this upward strike on the ball.)

Clearly, there are many styles to experiment with. But with all of them, it's vital that you keep your head still until you hear the ball rattle in the back of the hole, and hold your follow-through position. I always liked to concentrate on keeping my elbows close to the side of my body. A good way to do this is to trap a small water bottle under your right elbow as you practice. That prevents the putter wandering about and therefore helps in the process of grooving a consistent path. (Again, another reason many players prefer the left-hand-low grip, as it just seems to position the elbows better in relation to the body. Through the stroke, the arms work back and forth on a "rail.")

Does the putter work best moving straight back and through or following a gentle curve? Well, that depends. Unless you choose to manipulate the course of the putter with independent arm, hand, and wrist action, the putterhead will trace a natural curve inside the ball-to-target line as it swings back and forth. Simple laws of physics dictate that. However, on short putts up to around 10 feet on a quick surface, I believe it's quite legitimate to work on keeping the putterhead pretty much square to a relatively straight path, back and through. (In fact, in 1990 I played with great success my square-to-rotate stroke. It was square back with a very slight inside path line. Rotate, face open, and hold: an "anti-pull stroke." I draped my right index finger down the grip to control this rotation. This was the feeling I experienced, though in reality the putterface was traveling square-to-square, tracking the line of the putt.) At the speed you're trying to roll the ball, such is the length of stroke where a deviation would be negligible. It will move only fractionally inside of the ball-to-target line. So if picturing that straight line track back and through helps you hole putts, use it.

Visualize the angle of attack and the way the ball rolls for the initial few inches on that line. I went through a period in my career when I believed in straight back and through, and at the same time worked on de-lofting the putter through impact to give me a positive strike on the ball. Let's say my putter had 4 degrees of loft on the face—my mind-set was to bring it back to the ball at just 3 degrees, to de-loft the putter a little bit as I released it. To do this, I firmed up my left wrist and had a real sense of pulling the putter through the ball. It worked for a while, and it's a great way to create that soft lag in the transition from backswing to through-swing.

In the run-up to the 1992 British Open at Muirfield, I developed this technique with what I called a "brush" stroke. I would make my practice stroke with the objective of brushing the grain of the grass at impact—the key being to feel the resistance of the grass as you

literally brush the green. I would then make my real stroke looking for the same lag and acceleration through the putt *without* touching the green. Not only did this routine give me a positive focus in my pre-putt routine, but it also added a great feel and tempo to the stroke.

Conventional, reverse-handed, the flute, the piccolo, the pencil: Find the grip that gives you the most reliable stroke! These days, there really are no rules, and so you have carte blanche to experiment to find what works for you. Even if it works just for a brief period of time, then you find something new. Anything! On tour these days there are so many styles to choose from that players always have an alternative, which keeps the mind interested and fresh. Rather than sitting in the clubhouse moaning about the six three-putts you had, go out and tinker with all of the different grips, the belly putter, the long putter. Run the gamut. Rather than playing with anxious thoughts of missing, find a new style that requires a fresh way of thinking, and give your game a new lease on life.

PUT ALL OF that hard work to the test. Find a hole that is cut on a slight incline and circle four balls around it, at the points of a

compass. Start with short ones, two to three feet. Take a look at each putt, just as you would on the course, and then hole as many as you can in succession. Set a goal for yourself and try to beat it. Challenge your nerve. When I do this, I concentrate mostly on keeping my head still and trying to stroke the ball positively into the hole. I don't believe in babying putts. If you dribble the ball,

then the slight imperfections in the green are liable to throw your putts off line. I don't believe in ramming them in, either. Phil Mickelson bemuses me with the speed at which he often tries to hole these three- to five-footers. At that speed the line has to be 100 percent perfect—no more than a ball-width either side of the center line at the back of the cup, or you power lip-out. In our TV coverage we have access to some fascinating statistical analysis that tells us that when it comes to holing putts, dead weight wins! In other words, rolling the ball at a speed that sees it finish no more than 8 to 10 inches beyond the hole gives it the best chance of falling in. So you have to learn how to focus your attention in such a way that you are able to control perfectly the speed of delivery and the quality of your strike. I looked either at a specific spot or dimple on the ball or a blade of grass immediately behind it—and focused on that through the entirety of the stroke. Again, this is all about experimenting to establish your own preference. Some players look at a spot on

top of the ball; others have been known to close their eyes and "see" the putt in their mind. When I faced a short putt on mega-fast greens, I would often look at my right thumbnail and move it one inch back, one inch through. My thinking was that it's easier to control my thumbnail than the putter head!

THE TEMPO OF the stroke is critical. More short putts are missed because of a lack of tempo than

EXPERIMENT with the way you release the putter. If your putterface has 4 degrees of loft, imagine 3 degrees returns to the ball at impact. A sense of pulling through with the left hand will assist you.

anything else. So as you work on holing out, try to feel that your hands and the putterhead work at the same speed. Count to yourself "one-two" to establish your personal beat. Match your stroke to the rhythm of your breathing pattern. Take a gentle inhale and

exhale in time with your practice stroke, and then replicate that for real. The ability to control your breathing is a vital aspect of controlling your physical actions. Good breathing technique can help you to settle the nerves and quiet the mind—which will quiet your body.

"Acting as if..." can be a powerful mind tool. Copying a player whose style you admire can often boost your confidence and simply get your mind focused less on what you may have been doing wrong and more on positive images of doing something right. Think of the players who make holing-out look so easy: Australia's Aaron Baddeley makes a couple of practice swings perpendicular to the line of the putt and then walks straight in and hits the ball. No fuss, no bother. Luke Donald is the pro's pro—methodical in everything he does—and he swings the putter with the same metronome-like tempo he displays en route to the green. His stats will blow your mind. In 2011 he played more than 600 holes on tour without a three-putt. That tells you all you need to know about the importance of tempo. Tiger uses a very orthodox stroke, stands fairly tall, and creates a pure pendulum motion; he's at his best when he allows the toe of the putter to release for a solid strike.

Watch and learn from the players who rely on holing these "clutch" putts for a living. And don't be afraid to call on their services when you need a little help. Try it as you work on your stroke: Step into the ghost of a great player you would expect to make the putt for you, and make his or her style your own.

TEMPO IS THE KEY to a repeating stroke. Whether you favor de-lofting the face or allowing the putter to release naturally, say the words out loud as you practice: "ONE-TWO" as you swing the putterhead back and forth.

NARROW YOUR FOCUS, WIDEN THE TARGET

HERE'S A GREAT drill that does wonders for your confidence before teeing off. Find a straight six-footer, and create the chalk line. Then stick a tee into the green about three or four inches inside that line. Now spend a couple of minutes going through your routine and putting balls at that tee. When you've hit it three times in succession, place the ball on the chalk line and hole the putt. After you've been focusing on that tee, the hole will look enormous, and you'll simply make your stroke and pour the ball into the hole without fail. It's great for your confidence.#

VICTORY at the
Home of Golf, Open
Championship at
St Andrews, 1990.

RUN THE RAIL FOR SQUARE IMPACT

OUT ON THE course during a round of golf, it's very easy to lose touch with what square alignment looks and feels like, especially if you're prone to poor shoulder alignment in the full swing. That will be reflected in your putting setup. So take advantage of the opportunity to set up to a shaft (or a flagstick) whenever you have a moment during a round, and remind yourself of this key fundamental. Placing the sole of your putter on top of the shaft helps you to appreciate a true *square* alignment, and you can then monitor the path of the putterhead as you swing it back and forth. Remember, the momentum of the stroke comes from the upper body (which is why

you need those shoulders to be square). Following the logic of a natural stroke, the putter should trace a gentle arc inside going back, returning square at impact, and then travel inside once more on the way through. Some players like to make a natural backswing, running slightly on the inside, while keeping the face square to the line as they release it through. That's another option to think about. I used to like releasing the putter freely inside-to-square-to-inside on the longer putts, and would often think inside-to-square and through inside ten feet or so. I would imagine a pair of eyes on the putterface and keep them staring at my aim point as I held my follow-through.#

THE LONG OPTIONS

IT MAY BE THE SOLUTION YOU'RE LOOKING FOR . . .

KEEGAN BRADLEY'S victory in the 2011 PGA Championship represented the major breakthrough for the long putter. With his tremendous U.S. Open win at Olympic Club in 2012, Webb Simpson underlined the effectiveness of the belly-style that is increasingly de rigueur among those who use the long putter. There are a significant number of tour players who not only experiment in practice but actually flip back and forth between the regular length and a longer flatstick. If I were on tour today, I think I might try out a belly-style putter, at least to train and groove a repeating stroke on the practice green, even if I didn't use it on the course. I still prefer the feel of a conventional putter and stroke. But there are undoubtedly benefits attached to rehearsing with the longer model, especially the way in which the long putter encourages you to involve your chest in turning gently back and through. For best results, anchor the putter grip just left of your belly button. There's nothing wrong with that if it helps to keep your stroke fresh and your confidence sailing when you get out on the course. Perhaps more than any other player, Australia's Adam Scott exemplifies the way in which finding new confidence in this department carries into every other aspect of the game. The way he knocks in the four- to eight-footers today only reminds you of the number he missed in previous years and the damage that did to his ability to go low. Anchoring the grip enables him to trace a perfect natural path, like opening and closing a door.

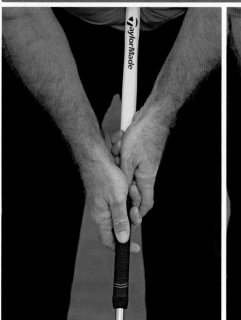
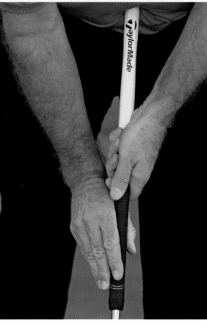

THE ADVANTAGE of the belly putter—however you choose to hold it—is that it involves the chest in turning back and through in tandem with the hands and arms.

MAKE EVERY PUTT A STRAIGHT PUTT TO YOUR AIM POINT

ONLY THROUGH experience can you learn the art of reading the contours of a green correctly. It's not easy to teach through the pages of a book, but if we were to spend some time on the green, I would certainly emphasize the fact that no matter how many contours and subtle breaks you have to negotiate on the way to the hole, your job is to see every putt as a straight putt. What I mean by that is you have to visualize the line all the way to the hole and identify the point at which the ball will first begin to break (just like the graphics we use in our TV broadcasts to illustrate the perfect line on a breaking putt). That aim point becomes your target. As you then go about setting up to the ball, aiming the putterface and so on, all you should be thinking about is rolling the ball over that point at your chosen speed.

Pace is the governing factor when it comes to reading a line. The harder you hit a putt, the less it will take the break; hit the ball too softly, and it will fall miserably off line. As I mentioned just a moment ago, all the evidence today would suggest that a putt running more or less to dead weight has the best chance of falling in; the ideal pace is that which would send the ball about a foot beyond the hole should it miss.

A point often overlooked is that on a curling putt the center of the hole moves. Think about it. If you study the line of a hard-breaking left-to-right putt, you'll see the ball entering the hole from the left edge (as you look at it). If the middle of the hole is normally represented by 6 o'clock on a clockface, that left-to-right slope could make the effective center close to 9 o'clock. It's vital you keep this in mind.

In the photo you see here, I've used a couple of tees to indicate what I've identified as my "aim point" on this left-to-right putt—at the ideal pace this is the initial line I want the ball to take on its way to the hole. A simple drill such as this one helps you get in the mode of looking for the "apex" of a breaking putt and learning to roll the ball at a speed that favors the high or "pro" side. Release the putter and roll the ball confidently on the high side, so that it always has a chance of falling in. On most continents, gravity works only in that direction. It's a lost cause if the ball runs out of steam on the low side of the cup.

DRILL

HOW TO FINE-TUNE TECHNIQUE AND FEEL

HERE'S AN ENTERTAINING drill that will help you tune in to the speed of the greens on a particular day. Starting 15 feet from the hole, string out a line of balls up to a distance of 60 feet or so, as I have done here. Begin with the ball closest to the hole. The key is to study the behavior of each putt as you roll it toward the hole and use that feedback to judge the perfect weight of each subsequent putt as you work down the line. This is all about your *feel* for distance, matching the length and the rhythm of your stroke to roll the ball a dead weight to the hole. Vary your position on the green to test yourself on left-to-right- and right-to-left-breaking putts, both uphill and downhill. The feedback will be invaluable out on the course. I would do this with my eyes closed, and sometimes with just my left or right hand only. Have fun. This is one of those drills that can become quite addictive, and the more you practice, the better your feel will be for both distance and break.#

LAG PUTTING

LENGTHEN YOUR STROKE AND ROLL THE BALL

ONE THING ALL good putters have in common is the ability to judge distance and roll the ball a dead weight to the hole. They have genuine *feel*. Most three-putts occur as the result of poor distance control, racing an approach putt past the hole or leaving it miserably short. And so giving some thought to the pace at which you roll the ball on a green, lengthening your stroke to maintain a tempo that gives you a solid strike, is a *must*.

The golden rule to remember when you work on longer putts is that the speed at which you release and roll the ball must be determined by the length of your stroke. This is all about controlling momentum. For me, tempo is always the key factor (as it is in the game generally). A good putting stroke is made with the same unhurried rhythm, no matter how far you have to roll the ball. I make it a habit to swing the putterhead back and forth at a smooth, even pace, relaxing my arms and wrists to such an extent that my putter is encouraged to accelerate smoothly. The one thing you have to avoid is any suggestion of a "hit" with the wrists—you are looking for a rhythm that is gradual as it works from the shoulders, arms, and hands to the putter. On particularly slow greens, emphasize that "lag" in the wrists to add subtle increase in acceleration.

Simple thoughts inside your mind can translate into a repeating rhythm. Try saying "one-two" in time with your stroke—"one" as you take the putter away, "two" as you swing it through the ball. On mega-fast greens you might extend that to "O-N-E-T-W-O." I would often say "shoulders-shoulders" on a longer putt, as the words themselves seemed to fit with a longer stroke. On a short putt, the message might be "square-square." It makes no difference what you work on, just do all you can to place the emphasis on finding a tempo that repeats itself. I think about keeping the upper part of each arm nicely connected with the upper torso, which maintains tempo through the stroke as the shoulders just rotate slightly. Get the chest in motion, too. As we've explored elsewhere in the game, this all helps toward the feeling of the torso doing the work and governing tempo as the arms and torso work together as a guiding unit. Any tendency of the arms to work independently of the upper body, and your stroke goes AWOL.

JUST A ROUTINE JOB TO DO . . .

THE FIVE-FOOTER I left myself on the 18th green at Muirfield in the 1987 Open Championship was probably the most pressure-laden putt of my career. In the process of grinding out 17 straight pars, I had holed several putts of a similar distance. Then, to win my first major championship, I had to face "one of those."

I made that putt because I treated it like any other. I lined it up the same way I lined up any other short putt that day and made my customary practice strokes to the side of the ball. Flooding my mind were thoughts of tempo, and I reminded myself to keep my head still. The cardinal error on pressure putts is to change the way you play just because you happen to find yourself facing a critical shot or putt. As soon as you do that, you create tension. So don't check all angles

for break if normally a quick look from either side of the hole does the job; don't stand there and make a dozen practice strokes if normally you're happy with just one or two; don't freeze over the ball—see the putt, and hit it. Develop a routine and *stick to that routine*. And don't say to yourself, "Don't miss this!"

Once you have that line of the putt in your mind, it's all about doing the same thing you've done all day long . . . just doing it better! If you lose touch with your natural rhythm and start peeking at the hole, you're in trouble. Concentration plays a huge part. The great Jack Nicklaus always stood out in this respect. Watch footage of Nicklaus in his prime tournament years, and you'll be amazed by the way he seemed to enter his own little world stalking a putt. He immersed himself in a cocoon of concentration, and nothing could

break that spell. A phenomenal skill, and it comes out of practice and confidence as you hole putt after putt after putt. This trait is often what separates the good putters from the great ones, perhaps a single-figure player from the mid-handicap club golfer.

Ultimately, the key is to focus on a putt, blocking all else around you. In your mind you must learn to see the ball going into the hole even before you've hit it. I've never really bought into that advice of lagging a putt into a dustbin lid or three-foot circle; your thoughts should be on holing the putt (just as they should be on holing a chip shot). Even if it misses, you ought to be able to walk off every green satisfied that you did all you could to make the putt. I've hit plenty of perfect putts in my time that defied gravity. That's golf. Whatever grip, whatever style you use, keep your strategy simple and satisfy your half of the bargain: Once you have lined up a putt, trust your stroke and let it go. I used to say to myself, "What is your intention here? What do you want?" More than anything, I wanted to see the ball running down the line and into the hole—particularly the last few feet of its journey. Once I had that visual in my mind, I could then *feel* the putt down the line, aim the putt perfectly, and GO.

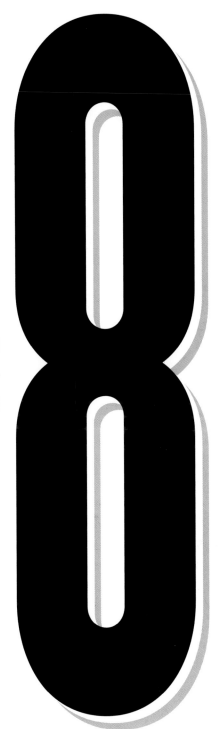

CHAPTER

CHIPPING AND PITCHING—

MY SHORT-GAME SYSTEM

NO MATTER HOW WELL YOU STRIKE THE BALL, **IT'S YOUR ABILITY TO TURN THREE SHOTS INTO TWO** THAT ULTIMATELY WILL MAKE OR BREAK YOUR SCORE.

THE HOURS I used to spend working from inside wedge distance to the hole could well be the time I miss the most since retiring from the tour. Okay, I miss the rush of being in the hunt on the weekend, dealing with pressure, coming down the stretch in the heat of a major championship, mouth dry, stomach churning. Those are the defining moments you live and breathe for as a player. But for sheer fulfillment, nothing beats a dedicated short-game practice session, chipping and pitching balls around a green and fine-tuning distance control with the wedges—the *scoring* shots.

This is the key area for every golfer who wants to see real improvement in his results: visualizing the trajectory of different wedge shots, feeling the ball on the clubface, and logging the specific sensations that help you to reproduce those skills out on the course and land the ball on a specific number.

While it's easy to get carried away with the distances the pros hit the ball off the tee these days, the real area of fascination, for me, remains this critical scoring range—wedge distance and in. That is where a golfer's true artistry is tested. And the beauty of the chipping, pitching, and wedge system that I am going to share with you lies in its simplicity and the ease with which I hope you will be able to build a reliable and satisfying family of short-game skills. Based on the same principles that I discussed in the full swing (and, for that matter, putting), the emphasis is once again on identifying a setup position that not only encourages you to synchronize the movement of your hands, arms, and body, but actually predetermines the quality of a good impact position.

When it comes to mastering trajectory and spin—the essence of the short game—we're looking specifically at controlling the speed of the club and the angle of attack (and shaft plane) as you strike the ball. These are the key variables to keep in mind as you survey the task in front of you. A lack of vision and creativity is usually what separates a good player from a great one, and at no other time in this game is your imagination more keenly tested than when you're approaching a green within wedge range. The art of visualizing the shot required to get the ball close to the hole is a skill that you can develop and nurture with practice. As you learn to associate feel with the techniques that I'm about to demonstrate, so you will learn to identify the *right club* at the *right time* in order to produce the ideal combination of trajectory, distance, bounce, and roll. The secret is to always be inventive—vary your position around the flag when you practice; *see* the perfect shot in your mind and challenge yourself to pull it off. See it fly . . . see it land . . . see it roll into the hole! Why not?

THE RHYTHM AND fluidity of your motion here are again paramount. Whether I was hitting full wedge shots, pitching, or chipping, once I had established a good setup position, I always paid attention to the role of my stomach, chest, and shoulders—specifically on the speed at which I would rotate them to control trajectory and landing distance. Even with a technique as simple as the one that we are about to explore in chipping, regulating tempo with the speed of your "core" rotation has a huge influence on the nature of the shot. In the wedge arena, especially on shots between 30 and 130 yards, I'd spend

a lot of time on my distance work, regulating the length of my swing to register my best distances with my chosen wedges. This is a *must* for anyone with real ambition in the game, and the simple "Clock-face Principle" of control that I always relied on can also help you take ownership of precise yardages. More on that a little later on.

I mentioned this briefly in Chapter 4, and I'm going to reiterate it here: Working on your skills with a wedge goes a long, long way toward improving the essential mechanics of your full swing. With a wedge in your hands, you're immediately aware of the quality of

ROTARY MOTION: Through the basics of chipping and pitching and all the way into the wedge game, the speed at which you rotate your body "core" is fundamental to your control of spin and distance.

wrist action necessary to hinge the club up in the backswing, to get it in "balance" (on plane). As ever, your ability to do this rests entirely on the quality of the fundamentals: the grip and setup position. The smarter you are here, the more consistently you can expect to repeat good technique and dial in a good impact position. So let's get to work, starting with one of the most versatile shots in golf.

THE "CHIP-PUTT"
A SIMPLE ONE-LEVER ACTION

LIFE IS FULL of tough decisions; choosing the right shot to play when you find your ball just a few feet from the edge of the green shouldn't be one of them. My philosophy is to get the ball on the deck and let it run like a putt as quickly as possible—a traditional "bump-and-run" style that I'd often play with this hybrid "chip-putt" technique, using the minimum of wrist action.

Simplicity itself, the trick here is to select the club that enables you to carry the ball just onto the putting surface—landing it a yard or so onto the green for a predictable first bounce—and then read the break to the hole like you would for a putt.

The setup reflects my intentions. With my regular putting grip, I first choke well down on the shaft (almost touching the metal), which not only enhances my control but also accommodates the club within a slightly "huddled" setup position. I play the ball well back, opposite the toe of my right shoe, my weight

just favoring my left side as I settle over what is a narrow and slightly open stance—my feet, knees, and hips all running left of my target line. My shoulders and forearms, meanwhile, are perfectly square to the line on which I intend to start the ball.

Look closely at this setup position, and you can *see* the nature of impact—it's dialed in. I call it "cheating impact." This aspect of your preparation is crucial to the way in which you approach all of the short-game skills I am going to share with you. Without the dynamic body rotation to clear the way for your hands and arms to release the club, you have to factor that in at address. Standing

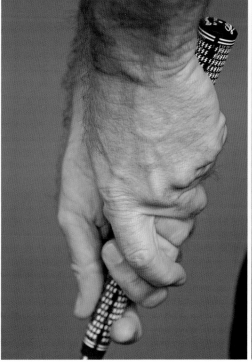

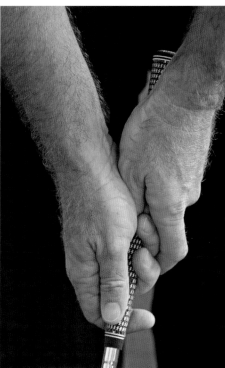

open to your line gives your lower body that head start, and also assists you in *releasing* the toe of the club freely, which will help you solidify the strike.

The stroke itself is a basic pendulum motion controlled—for me—by the right shoulder.

Maintaining a light grip pressure adds to the subtle "play" in my wrists as I change direction, but essentially the hands are passive throughout. I simply send my right shoulder up to the sky and then down toward the ball—that's it as far as the mechanics go!

Standing slightly open to the shot effectively takes the lower body out of the action, and while my knees ease slightly left as I swing through, my torso controls the stroke, with my arms and hands responding to the momentum of my upper body.

The sensation you're looking for is a gentle brushing of the grass as you clip the ball forward, so rehearse this with a few practice strokes. Feel the resistance of the grass and create the tempo necessary to play a positive shot.

This technique is so versatile that you can experiment with virtually every club in your bag. I'd suggest that you work initially with a span of three clubs—say, a 6-iron, an 8-iron, and a wedge. Switching between them at random will quickly teach you the relationship between trajec-

BASED ON THE SIMPLICITY of a basic pendulum-style putting stroke, the hybrid chip-putt technique is one of the most valuable shots to have in your repertoire around the green.

tory and roll on the green. When I play these shots, I aim to land the ball a yard or so onto the putting surface and focus on repeating a smooth "one-two" tempo, or simply say "up, down," keeping the clubhead fairly low to the ground back and through, creating a saucer-shaped swing path. With the relatively straight-faced 6-iron, the ball is quickly on the green and runs willingly toward the hole; the 8-iron flies a tad higher and runs a little less; while the wedge produces a softer type of shot that may only run out a few feet.

Take a bag of balls and experiment. A lot of tour players even reach for a lofted hybrid club when they need to play a straightforward bump-and-run—especially when playing into the grain, because it's a safe and effective recovery shot that gets the ball running willingly even with a relatively small stroke. But you do need to practice it. At the other end of the spectrum, using the same technique with your most lofted wedge produces a pop-up shot that might fly only a couple of yards and then stop on a dime. Go out and explore the possibilities. One more thing to keep in

STANDING IRON CLUBS almost vertically at the setup enables you to access the rounded toe of the blade and thus get to the bottom of the ball—another benefit of this versatile technique.

mind is that the more vertically you sit the iron clubs at address, the more you can take advantage of the rounded shape of the toe to get to the bottom of the ball when you have a particularly tough lie, especially on hard ground. Just be aware that striking the ball here tends to deaden impact, so you'll need to factor that into the equation. More food for thought.

GET IT ON THE GREEN AS QUICKLY AS YOU CAN . . .

DURING THE LATE 1970s and early '80s, Japan's Isao Aoki was a regular contender on the European Tour, and a popular one. His game was based entirely on feel for the angle of the clubface, and he possessed almost a sixth sense for visualizing the shots he needed to play. You couldn't take your eyes off him. I played with Isao many times, and watching him work his magic taught me one of the all-time short-game lessons: The "percentage shot" is the one that gets the ball on the green as quickly as possible, running at the hole just like a putt. His preference was to identify a landing area about a yard onto the putting surface, then select the club that gave him the desired combination of flight and roll according to the distance the ball had to travel to the hole. When there was a lot of green to work with, the "right club" might be a 5-iron, but to a really close pin, he'd take a lofted wedge. The thing that appeals to me is that all you have to control (all you *can* control) is the carry onto the green, which is why moving your landing spot as close to you as possible makes sense. This is smart thinking that reduces every single shot to nothing more complicated than thinking "landing spot, right club, and roll."#

THE CHIPPING ACTION
ADDING THE WRISTS, INCREASING SPEED

VIDEO LESSON:
THE ART OF CHIPPING
One of the most versatile scoring shots in golf also happens to be one of the easiest to perfect with a little know-how: Sit back and enjoy a master class as Nick takes you through the fundamentals of sound technique and shares a few tips that will help you to visualize the right shot at the right time.

I **LIKE THE WAY** the "chip-putt" teaches you the simplicity of the chipping principle. But it is primarily for shots around the very edge of the green with a landing range of just a handful of yards. As you move a little farther out, the length of your swing must reflect the distance you need to fly the ball through the air. The key is knowing how to adjust your setup position so you're able to blend good technique with feel, and really, there are just two small changes to make. First, you need to stand a little taller at address, so that your arms are free to hang

in front of your body (but at the same time maintain that brushing contact with your upper arms and chest). Second, revert to your regular full-swing grip.

Before we look at the shot itself, though, here's a quick experiment you should try: Look what happens if I take a handful of balls and spend a few minutes tossing them underarm toward a hole, aiming to replicate the flight and roll of a good chip shot. Without thinking about my alignment, my

body has responded to the challenge: I've opened my body up to the target—that gives me a good view of the "shot"—and my weight automatically favors the forward foot. With my eyes focused on where I want the ball to land and go, releasing the ball with a natural underarm motion sees my right arm and wrist move in harmony with my upper body, and as I turn through to arrive at the finish, my body structure is per-

fectly balanced. It's not so much a body action to speak of—it's more a *momentum* from the stomach and the chest, while the right forearm *feels* the distance. Look how far through your body travels, rotating and opening up to face the target—a natural motion that hints at good golf technique. The key now is to hold on to those feelings as you work on developing a back-and-through chipping action with the same fluency and balance; don't deny yourself that same freedom in the stroke.

The most noticeable aspect of the setup is the fact that my lower body is significantly open to my target line. Again, the nature of this shot is such that you simply don't create the body dynamic to clear the left side out of the way through impact, so you have to take care of that at the setup. "Cheating impact" in this fashion enables you to focus on the top half of your body as you rotate back and through, your shoulders, forearms, wrists, and hands (in that order) controlling the flowing motion of the club. Adding that height to my posture allows the arms to hang freely, placing the hands in a comfortable position beneath the sternum. My favorite reminder—*knees*—adds to the overall balance as I flex them gently and lean toward the target.

Once you've effectively preset a good impact position, the key to the swing is that your shoulders, arms, and hands—*in that order*—do all the work. It's a chain reaction. With that connection (between your upper arms and chest) established at the setup, when your shoulders move, your arms and hands follow; there is a sense of total upper-body awareness, feeling the weight of the arms moving in conjunction with

the bigger muscles in the torso. I love the sensation of controlling tempo with the rotation of my stomach, which creates a lovely sense of *flow* as the arms and hands move in response to that core momentum. As long as you maintain a sensitive grip pressure, you should feel your wrists hinge gently to add a silky *lag* between backswing and downswing. That's the secret to a classic chipping action. Whether your swing is long or short, cultivating that "play" in the wrists enables you to regulate the speed of the clubhead through impact for ultimate ball control.

GRIPPING DOWN the shaft (*right*) is good practice in all aspects of the short game, as it immediately enhances your feel for the clubhead.

RHYTHM AND FLOW (*below*) are the hallmarks of a good chipping action, so encourage that "lag" in the wrists as you change direction and accelerate the club into the downswing.

CONTROL DISTANCE WITH TRAJECTORY

ENCOURAGING THE RIGHT FOREARM to rotate over the left lowers trajectory and encourages the ball to fly with right-to-left spin; to hold the clubface open for a higher shot, the right hand works beneath the left, maximizing loft on the clubface. Take this principle of control and experiment with both your chipping and your pitching technique.

VIDEO LESSON: HOW TO MANIPULATE FLIGHT
Simple adjustments in ball position and the way you rotate and release your arms and wrists can produce an array of controlled pitch shots. The key is to focus on "strike and flight," says Nick, as he shows you how to control trajectory and spin.

THE BETTER YOUR rhythm, the greater the scope this upper-body-controlled technique will give you. At every opportunity, take a bag of balls and work on developing this subtle art, cementing that connection between your upper arms and chest. Concentrate on making the same smooth stroke each time, and switch between clubs to vary the trajectory of your shots. Think in terms of controlling the length and speed of your swing with the rotary motion of your trunk—let your wrists hinge naturally to complement your overall rhythm, and hold your finish as you watch each shot unfold.

As you start exploring this technique, the logic of the setup position will become clear. The beauty of a neutral chipping action is that you're always working with the natural loft on the clubface. In fact, a good practice challenge is to look for and *see* the natural loft on the clubface returning to the back of the ball at impact—that really does sharpen your concentration. Start off five to ten yards from the edge of a green and run the numbers from an 8-iron all the way down to your wedges to get an idea of the flight-to-roll ratio each of the clubs gives you. Stick a tee in the green just a couple of yards onto the surface, and make that your focal point.

Study the behavior of each shot: the way the ball spins and checks on the second or third bounce, and the subsequent run-out to the hole.

When I used to practice these shots, I would work a system of using two ball positions (one normal and one farther back, opposite the toe of my right shoe) and two distinct tempos ("smooth-smooth" and "smooth-aggressive") to vary the height and spin of the shots that I could play with a single club. Mixing these variables, I could produce four different shots and landing speeds using one club—with very little change in the technique. Again, this simply illustrates the rich versatility that exists in this department of the game.

As you grow more confident, you can be more ambitious still and actually *work* the ball. Imagine you're playing a mini-draw, and encourage the rotation of your right forearm over the left as you release the club to the finish. Turning the toe over the heel produces overspin, which can be useful when you need to run the ball up a slope or control a shot into wind. In some cases, you may need the ball to check up a little more than normal, so work on a slicing action that produces

backspin. To do that, you'd play the ball a half or full ball forward in your stance and make a conscious effort to hold the clubface open through impact. This time you want your right hand working *beneath* the left. There is no crossover here. In fact, the feeling to have is that you pull the heel of the club across the ball with cut action, keeping your left wrist firm. (Remember what I've said about picturing a little piece of sandpaper on the face so that you really grip the ball.)

Trial and error is the only way to become a more educated golfer. You can vary the length and pace of your swing simply by adjusting the speed at which you rotate your stomach and the center of your chest. That's always been my preferred technique—it's like having a dial you can turn up or down to play shots that either amble slowly or run more quickly. The faster you move your middle, or core, the more speed you can put into the clubhead and the more the ball will want to run. Slow things down, and you get a softer, lazier shot. These are skills to practice, and skills that add a powerful dimension to your game.

TEST YOUR FEEL AND IMAGINATION

**VIDEO LESSON:
VALUABLE FEEDBACK**
Sharpen your powers of visualization with this simple line drill—a routine Nick relied on throughout his career, and one that's a lot of fun to work on around the practice green.

THE ART OF reading a chip shot and visualizing the solution to a problem is all part of the fun—and this drill teases you with a different proposition at every step up or down the "ladder." I used to do this sort of thing regularly during a tournament week to familiarize myself with the type of grass around the greens and the levels of spin I might be able to generate. (Of course, the exact type of shot you're able to play depends on the lie, and to make this realistic, I'd drop balls into place rather than sit each one up on a tuft of grass!) Assuming a good lie, I might see the ideal shot as being a lofted one with a 53- or 60-degree wedge, one that lands the ball a yard or so onto the green with sufficient spin to finish close. If a ball is sitting down, I would have to reevaluate, and perhaps play a bump-and-run–style shot, using the upslope to take off pace and buffer the ball on its way to the hole-side. Only practice can teach you to recognize the *right shot* at the *right time*, so put your touch—and your imagination—to the test.#

1. SET

2. STOMACH

MY 4 KEY MOVES TO SOLID WEDGE PLAY

YOU WILL IMPROVE your pitching action the next time you play if you focus on what I refer to as the four key moves to better and more consistent wedge play:

1. *Set:* This is one of the *musts* for a sound wedge technique: The clubhead needs to start moving relatively quickly in the backswing. The precise nature of the shot will determine the degree of attention you give this, but "setting" the wrists and gathering speed early is a sign of confidence with the wedge.

2. *Stomach:* I have always believed the easiest way to think about creating momentum, and to get all the components of the swing working *together,* is to focus on the rotation of the stomach. Working the arms and the stomach away in tandem sets up a wonderful rhythm and *togetherness* in the swing.

3. *Turn:* Just as important here in the wedge game as it is in the full swing, the reminder *turn* simply energizes the upper body and places the emphasis for control on the shoulders. On three-quarter to full swings with a wedge, the committed turning

of the upper body is important for tempo and accuracy and also gives you the best chance of returning the club through impact on the correct plane line.

4. *Through:* Your body language at the finish always reflects your intentions with a specific shot. The length and shape of the finish indicates where your focus lies—it could be the shoulders, the buttons on the shirt, arms, wrists, hips, or chest. It will vary according to the type of shot you're playing. And it is vital to the outcome.

3. TURN

4. THROUGH

FOR RHYTHM, THINK "STOMACH AND BUTTONS"

ONCE I'M READY to play, my thoughts are geared toward turning my upper body over the support of my knees and thighs, and working on setting the wrists to swing the club up in "balance" (more on that in a moment). Shots from this range are all about the arms and the upper body working together. With a premium on accuracy, I think in terms of repeating a half to three-quarter swing and controlling my acceleration through the ball with the rotary motion of my body (the big danger here being the body stops, the arms go). One of the swing thoughts I have used over the years is "stomach and buttons." I focus on turning my stomach away from the ball to create the backswing, and then try to finish with my shirt buttons facing the hole. That gets my center turning back and forth, which creates the momentum I need to get the

arms *swinging*. It also helps me to establish good rhythm—and for that fact alone it's a great comfort when stressed under pressure. For the sake of good balance, foot-work is kept to a minimum.

Focus on the initial sequence of motion. You don't want the hands to be overactive (the overall sense of control has to come from the "core"), but at the same time, you must use them to get the clubhead moving before the wrists, forearms, belly, and chest all get involved. When it all links together, you get

a wonderful sense of coordination and flow, the rhythm of the overall swing enhanced with a subtle "lag" in the wrists as you ease into the downswing.

Just as we explored in the full swing, the better your body action, the more you can play this shot with the forearms and the hands. And the more you learn to associate control with the rotary motion of your body, the more easily you will control flight and distance. One of the tricks I liked to use was imagining that I was

playing the shot standing inside a tube, so that I really did have to focus 100 percent on turning about a consistent spine angle: knees, hips, chest, and shoulders, all rotating precisely, just gently touching the inside of the tube. (I was always conscious of maintaining my "levels," a good indicator being the consistency of my belt line.) Another good sensation is that of the upper triceps resting and working closely with the top of your chest—that always helps to keep the movement *connected*.

DRILL

HINGE THE CLUB UP IN "BALANCE"

HERE IS PROBABLY the best lesson I can give you for wedge technique (and it's one that will also work wonders for your full swing). We're talking again about the full and correct "setting" of the wrists in the preliminary stages of the backswing, so that the club swings up on a good plane, or is "balanced," as I prefer to think about it.

The proper hinging of the wrists serves as the go-between in a good swing; it blends the movement of the arms and the body to get the club swinging up in balance. Any time you have a few minutes to spare, pick up a wedge and rehearse this action. Relax your hands and forearms and look for this checkpoint: Swing your left arm across the chest and get the wrists fully hinged by the time they reach the halfway stage—really *crank* the right hand back on itself and look for this "cupping" at the back of the left wrist. When you

get this action working correctly, the club swings up in plane, with the shaft gently angled back as you observe your position "down the line."

A simple exercise can help you appreciate the sensation of up-ending the club to find this balance point. Grab a wedge, grip it well down the shaft, and hold it gently between your thumb and forefinger on the right hand. Grip it as lightly as you can, so that you really feel the weight of the clubhead on the end of the shaft, and then simply allow the club to swing up until it finds this natural balance point, when the right hand reaches about hip high. When you hinge the right wrist correctly, the club will feel light in your hands as it reaches this near-vertical position.

Once you have the knack of setting the wrists correctly, you can focus on blending the arms, as your swing is a product of the momentum of that body rotation. And the better your body works, the more it'll feel like your forearms and wrists are liberated to *feel* the shot. I really do believe this is the one time in the game when the shaft plane rules *everything*—and practicing this technique will hone what are the essential moving parts to repeat a golf swing. So come back to that "pencil-grip" exercise regularly, identify where your balance point is, and then let the club find its natural plane as you blend your arm-swing with body motion.#

DISTANCE WORK
THE "CLOCKFACE PRINCIPLE"

NOW THAT YOU have the basis of good technique, let me share one of the most effective visuals that I used to regulate the length and tempo of my swing in this scoring zone. Ultimately, good wedge play boils down to strike, trajectory, and distance control, and I found I could very easily consolidate these variables simply by matching the length of my swing to the numbers on a clockface. Putting this into practice couldn't be any simpler: The objective is to marry up the length of your backswing with the equivalent position in the follow-through, so that you're able to differentiate between specific swings. To give you an example of the way this works, my 9 o'clock to 3 o'clock swing with a 60-degree wedge gives me a shot that flies 50 yards. If I extend that swing to a 10 o'clock backswing and 2 o'clock finish, it'll go 60 yards; 11 o'clock to 1 o'clock would give me 70 yards; and the max with a 60-degree wedge, a "comfortable full swing,"

would give me 85 yards.

You get the idea. Matching your arm-swing to numbers on an imaginary clockface gives you access to a scoring system that's easy to grasp, and one that you can further develop with a simple adjustment in tempo. I work on the principle that the majority of my scoring shots are played with a "smooth" tempo, but I also work on what I call my "aggressive-smooth" tempo to increase my speed through the ball and add

a handful of yards (and a little more backspin) to the regular numbers. But the key, always, is that these swings are made with the emphasis on *control*. This is not an exercise to find out how far you're able to fly your wedges with maximum effort; it's about establishing your "best" and most consistent landing distances with a controlled and measured swing. (Whether or not you swing *exactly* to these positions on a clockface is not important. The key to this

sort of technique is that you learn to identify with a series of distinct positions that provide *you* with a personal scale.)

Clearly, the message here is that you have to go out and discover your personal matrix of "best" yardages with the span of wedges in your bag. This all boils down to personal preference in the makeup of your set. I carry a 47-degree pitching wedge, a 53-degree gap, and a 60-degree sand wedge; out on tour, a lot of players are sacrificing a long iron to include four wedges (typically 47, 52, 56, and 60), which reflects the importance of this part of the game in terms of scoring potential. It's standard practice now for a tour player to spend a lot of time measuring precise yardages and checking spin rates with the help of TrackMan and other such devices. The technology really is quite astonishing, and whether you have access to this sort of equipment, or use a laser range-finder in your own distance work, gathering this information and noting it in your yardage book is the first step down the road toward a more professional course strategy. Trust me, there's nothing better for your confidence than knowing *exactly* how far you fly each of your wedges with a certain swing.

WEDGE WORKS

HOW TO FINE-TUNE DISTANCE AND FLIGHT CONTROL

ONE OF MY favorite attacking shots was the 105-yard 53-degree wedge with my 11 o'clock to 1 o'clock swing. That's the range I used to go looking for out on the course. On a very short par 4, I'd calculate the tee shot required to leave myself with 105 to the flag; similarly, if a par 5 was out of reach in two shots, I'd lay up to the 105-yard mark. Why? Because the softer bounce on my 53-degree wedge gave me the consistency in the strike that enabled me to land the ball on that 105-yard number.

Of course, nothing in this game is absolute, and every time you play you'll encounter situations that require further manipulation to fine-tune both distance and trajectory. One of the easiest adjustments you can make is shortening your grip. Try going down the shaft progressively one, two, or even three inches. With every step you take, you're effectively shorten-

THE BETTER your body action, the more you will enjoy involving the forearms and the hands in controlling the nature of the strike.

BALANCE IS VITAL in the process of synchronizing your arm and body motion to the finish.

ing the length of the club, which means that without having to adjust your swing, you automatically diminish clubhead speed through the ball and produce a shot that flies a bit less, and lower, each time. I always thought this a terrific ploy under pressure, the beauty of this method being that once you've made the necessary adjustment to your grip, you can still make a full

turn and be aggressive through the ball. (When I was a young professional just starting out, British golfing legend Sir Henry Cotton urged me to push this system to its absolute limits. He would get me so far down on the grip that my right hand would be on the metal—"Don't be afraid to go onto the steel," Sir Henry would urge me. Proof again that the limits to your versatility are set only by the confines of your imagination.)

Experimenting with the pressure in certain fingers can have a significant bearing not only on your feel for playing a certain type of shot, but also on the outcome. If I want to hit a lower, *punchier* type of shot, I'll always tighten my hold in the last three fingers on my left hand. If I want to hit a higher, floating type of shot, I will relax the left hand and fingers, and instead feel pressure in the *trigger* unit of the right hand.

Another way to vary trajectory is to experiment with the ball position within your stance. If I want to lower the trajectory of my shots, I set up with the ball back in my stance, and let my weight

favor the left side (be careful not to exaggerate this). In the swing itself I then feel my upper body dominating the shot. I focus on making a full shoulder turn and swing the club more around my body than normal, a little flatter and with more arm rotation, both back and through. That rotation is felt at impact, as the clubhead turns over the ball and sends it flying with a low draw. (Thoughts

of keeping your right shoulder high through impact further assist you in "trapping" the ball for that satisfying ball-turf strike.) I finish the job with a compact, three-quarter-length follow-through.

Taking this to extremes, one of my favorite attacking shots is the "punch-pitch," an aggressive shot that flies with a fairly low trajectory and stops quickly on the second or third bounce as the backspin kicks in. This technique involves "holding off" the club-face through impact to trap the

WITH YOUR WEIGHT favoring your left side and a real sense of striking down and through the ball, you can enjoy playing this aggressive "punch-pitch," holding off the club-face to diminish the natural loft.

ball between the clubface and the turf with a descending strike. It's a great weapon to have, one that you can enjoy when making a three-quarter-length swing with your wedges, primarily to hold the ball on line in any sort

of head- or crosswind. And the more I wanted to spin the ball, the more I would focus on pulling a little more sharply across it with my left hand. (Remember that sandpaper-on-the-clubface visual!)

AGAIN, I ALWAYS keep in mind this concept of "cheating impact" as I prepare to play this shot, my knees choreographing the setup, weight favoring the left side, ball back of center. The movement of my arms is again governed by the engine of my shoulders and upper body, usually with nothing more than a compact three-quarter backswing. I focus on hinging my wrists to get the club swinging up in balance, and then hold on to that angle between my hands and the shaft through the hitting area, de-lofting the club further, punching the ball forward. This is best observed from the target (that is, me hitting over the camera), as the hips rotate aggressively, inviting my hands and forearms to pull sharply across and left of the target line to the finish. This is what is meant by "holding off" a shot; the clubhead is not allowed to pass the hands as I unwind my upper body to a controlled three-quarter finish, with my chest facing the target. There's no harm done by watching your strike and divot through impact before letting your head turn to follow the ball flight.

To accentuate loft and play a higher shot, I simply open my stance, settle my weight more evenly between the feet, and move the ball forward. These adjustments automatically place my hands back a touch and increase the effective loft on the clubface. The key in the swing is then to make sure that you still see your left shoulder come under your chin before releasing the arms and club to your max. The follow-through position this time is noticeably fuller and higher, and the body language again reveals the intention behind the shot.

If you exaggerate these adjustments to play a high ball, you soon enter the realm of the so-called "parachute lob," and there aren't many more thrilling escape shots. You need a good cushion of grass to play this shot, but if conditions are in your favor, you can make the ball climb almost vertically and stop very quickly.

Phil Mickelson is the undisputed master of this shot, and it's a skill worth practicing for the sheer confidence that pulling it off will

LOFTY AMBITION: Setting the wrists early in the backswing maintains an open clubface, giving you the green light to release the right arm on the way down and slide the open clubface under the ball.

give you. With your most lofted wedge, set up to the ball as if you were playing a regular sand shot, with an open stance and an even more open clubface. Get the shaft of the club pointing to your belt buckle, with the hands fractionally behind the ball. That adds even more loft. Once you're comfortable, focus on setting your wrists fairly early in the backswing—really crank them up to create this

"cupping" in the left wrist that confirms the face is wide open. As you start down, you want your left shoulder to move away from your chin, soft and level (maybe even working slightly down) to give you the sensation of shallowing out your right arm to swing the open clubface under the ball. This is all about the bounce striking the ground, not the leading edge, and you only achieve that with the release of the right arm that enables you to accelerate the open clubface underneath the ball. Go after the sensation of releasing the clubhead *past* the hands. Folding your left arm away quickly in the follow-through, keeping that left elbow close to your side, will help you to achive this (just as it does playing a splash shot in the sand). Oh, and good luck!

Work on these thoughts while you're practicing and find out just how versatile—and accurate— you can be with your short irons. These are the skills you'll need when facing difficult, ever-changing conditions while shooting for the flagstick.

VIDEO LESSON: DISTANCE WORK
Turning to one of the most important scoring shots in the game, from 40 to 120 yards, Nick explains the key elements of wedge technique designed to help you perfect your strike, and then shares his thoughts on the various methods with which you can fine-tune your distance control.

CHAPTER

LEARN TO LOVE THE SAND

IF RECOVERING FROM THICK GREENSIDE ROUGH IS HARD WORK, PLAYING OUT OF THE SAND IS A DAY AT THE BEACH **ONCE YOU LEARN TO APPRECIATE THE UNIQUE NATURE OF IMPACT.**

HE SOUNDS of golf have always intrigued and inspired me. When I started out, the clatter of spikes from the locker room to the course was guaranteed to get the juices flowing—that unmistakable theme-tune announcing the game was about to begin. Opening a sleeve of balls still has that sense of anticipation about it. Ripping and tightening the Velcro on your glove is the satisfying signal of intent as you survey a shot, and there's nothing more dramatic than the speed and the compression of ball-then-turf as a top player strikes a long iron. I can remember my father taking me to the British Open at Royal Troon in 1973,

and me being mesmerized by the sound of Tom Weiskopf's drives piercing the air as the ball rifled off into the distance. (Has there ever been a better sound than the *thwack* of persimmon on balata?)

Happily, the march of technology hasn't dulled the airwaves entirely. For me, one of the greatest sounds (and feelings) in the game is experienced here in the sand. And recognizing the speed, the fizz, and the sheer *gusto* of a well-executed greenside bunker shot is elemental as we turn our attention to one of the most valuable skills in golf: the splash shot.

The key here lies in developing the confidence to accelerate the open face of your sand wedge beneath the ball to produce a shot that comes out softly with spin. And the secret is that you simply have to keep the clubhead moving, *surfing* it through the sand at speed as you accelerate to a finish. It's rather like playing a good pitch shot, and we're reminded here of why working on these specific skills is so beneficial for your full swing—you are cementing the relationship between your hands, arms, and upper body over the balance and stability of your lower body. But the feeling here, with your feet shuffled into the sand for traction and stability, is that it's all arms and upper body.

In many respects, sand play remains a bastion of golf's tradition, and the sound of a well-played shot hasn't changed since the

day Gene Sarazen came up with the idea of welding solder to the lower back of his wedge so that it sat lower than the leading edge, a modification he made in 1932 after observing the way the flaps on the wings of a light aircraft pushed wind down to help the plane go up. Sarazen's genius (quite apart from that 4-wood he holed for double-eagle on the 15th hole at Augusta en route to winning the 1935 Masters) was to similarly create a flange that would give the sand iron "lift," or "bounce," as it has become popularly known. Opening the face of the sand wedge progressively increases this unique characteristic of what is a specialist club, and as long as you fulfill your half of the bargain—that is, maintain speed through impact—you literally splash the ball out.

So go out and have some fun working on this part of your game. There's no good reason why bunkers should make you fearful or cause you any problems. With a few simple drills, you can learn to recognize the sound and the feel of a well-executed sand shot. And it's addictive. The moment you experience the sensation and hear the sound of that first perfect sand shot, you will want to repeat it over and over again. And that's a good thing. Practicing your bunker play will make you a more aggressive wedge player because of the way you release the club and commit to striking *through* the shot.

LET THE CLUBHEAD TEACH YOU GOOD BUNKER TECHNIQUE

I COULD SPEND HALF an hour giving you the full rundown on the details that I try to incorporate in good sand technique, but it wouldn't add up to a hill of beans compared to the feelings you can experience for yourself with a simple DIY lesson. Next time you go out to practice, try this experiment: Spend the first two or three minutes swinging your sand wedge with your right hand only. Forget about a ball and focus instead on thumping the heavy flange through the sand. To do this, you'll first need to swivel the club through the fingers of your right hand to open the clubface. (If pointing the lead-ing edge up vertically at 12 o'clock is your starting position, rotate it clockwise in your fingers until the leading edge points to around 2 o'clock.) Close your right-hand grip with the face in that posi-tion, stand slightly open to the direction of your swing, and then focus on swinging the clubhead freely—feel the acceleration as you release your right hand, and listen to the sound you make.

As I mentioned a moment ago, the secret to playing these shots lies in delivering this speed through the sand. When you release your right hand correctly, the clubhead accelerates and that open clubface skims through the sand, producing a wonderfully distinctive sound. It won't take you long to recognize the thrust of a good shot. The more you open the clubface, the more the bounce lifts the clubhead up and out of the sand—and the more satisfy-ing the experience. Hold the club lightly in your fingers and you get a real sense of that acceleration as you let the club release past the hand. That's the critical element of good bunker play—clubhead *speed*—and it comes from that ac-celeration and release of the right hand. That's what gives you the sound of success. Without even thinking about technique, you are on the way to being a good bunker player.

THE REGULAR SAND SHOT
ROTATE AND RELEASE

IN TERMS OF your ability to keep a score going, the greenside bunker shot could be the most important recovery in golf. As simple as it sounds, the way you form your grip holds the key. To access that magical element of

AS YOU SETTLE into position, check that the butt-end of the club points directly up toward your belly button, and then adjust the loft on the open clubface before you complete your grip.

bounce, you need to open the face of your sand wedge, and you must do this *before* completing your grip. More on that in a moment.

For a regular sand shot, I'd stand anywhere up to 30 degrees open to the target, and settle down with my weight just favoring my left side. I flex the knees and gently shuffle my shoes into the sand until my body is nicely anchored. (Good bunker play is all about the wrists, arms, and upper body; there is no weight shift to speak of and no need for any fancy footwork. But your body must gently unwind and get through to face the target.) One of the best tips I've ever been given is to aim the butt-end of the club toward your belly button, which places the arms and hands in a nice neutral position in relation to the torso. The ball is played opposite the left instep. I then swivel the club through my fingers until the face is open in relation to my body, but square to open with the line to the flag. Once I'm happy with the po-

sition of the clubface, I complete my grip and get ready to play.

Having effectively preset a good impact position (we're "cheating" impact again!), making the swing is relatively easy. You simply follow the line of your body. The clubhead leads, wrists and forearms rotate while the chest turns; on the way down, you reverse the sequence—chest turns, forearms and wrists release, and the clubhead skims through the sand. The key is to focus your eyes on a spot in the sand a couple of inches behind the ball—that's your point of entry—and then thump the sand with the bounce of the club

(not the leading edge) on the way to your finish position. Keep your arms and wrists relaxed as you turn your shoulders back and through, and listen for that distinct sound as you release the club through to a balanced finish. Hold it as you watch the ball land softly on the green.

There's no harm done if you watch the sand explode through impact. Don't make the mistake of setting up to that entry point in the sand and then looking at the ball as you make your swing. You

have to be 100 percent focused on exactly where you want the flange on your sand wedge to make contact with the sand. Developing good technique is all about being able to control the bottom of your swing arc, so focus on what you're aiming to hit. Once you've identified that spot in the sand, you can almost forget about the ball.

Be careful, also, that the ball doesn't creep back in your stance and the hands go forward. When that happens, it's impossible to release the club properly, and you lose the ability to accelerate and get the clubhead swinging past the hands at speed. So keep

an eye on these basics. You'll get the best results with the ball just forward of center, so that you give yourself time to extend your right arm fully as you skim the clubhead through the sand. This is all about speed in the clubhead—that's how you generate the friction that creates backspin.

As you become more confident with this basic technique, you can experiment with the degree to which you open the clubface and the speed with which you deliver it through the sand. Regulating speed will also help give you a feel for distance control. You have all this to discover. If a pin is cut tight to the bunker, you can lay the face wide open and take a shallow cut to generate a soft shot with spin; if you need the ball to travel a little farther, you would square the face a little bit and focus on adding a little more speed. You have to mix these ingredients together to discover what's possible. Just remember that whether you're being cute or aggressive, the clubhead must always accelerate through the sand beneath the ball.

YOUR FOCUS throughout must be 100 percent on your entry point in the sand. Thump it with confidence, and the ball will surf out.

FIND THE LINE

TO HAVE ABSOLUTE control in the sand, you need to get a feel, an awareness, for the bottom of your swing arc. And there's no more effective way of doing that than spending time in a bunker working on the line drill. This has become one of my "standards," for the way in which it quickly lets you know how effectively you're repeating a good swing and taking a shallow and consistent cut of sand. If there's a rake handy, press it into the sand to create a distinct straight line, and then spend a few minutes working your way along it, with your focus on making this your point of entry. Set up to the line just as you would set up to a ball, so it bisects your left heel, opening the clubface to utilize the bounce. Then simply work your way down the line, trying to thump it every single time.

VIDEO LESSON: THUMP THE LINE
Forget about the ball. . . . The most effective way to boost your confidence in a bunker is to spend a little time relating your swing to a line in the sand, learning to deliver the "bounce" on the sand wedge consistently. Nick has the details as he enjoys one of his all-time favorite bunker drills.

When I do this, I remind myself of the need to get the grip of the club pointing at my belly button, while also making a point of leveling my shoulders (a common mistake being to "cramp" the right side of the body; raising the right shoulder will help you to get the ball airborne more easily and hit it higher). It's then all about the rotation of your upper body controlling the swinging of your arms, until you can thump that line every time. After four or five swings, you should be looking at a neat row of divots, each one starting bang on that line. (Simple diagnostics: When the club strikes the sand before the line, you are most likely using too much independent arm action; when you strike beyond the line, you are overusing your chest and upper body and looking up through impact.)

Vary the length of your backswing and match it with the follow-through to regulate your speed and acceleration through impact. That's both your volume and your distance control. To fine-tune the distance you land the ball, try also gripping down the shaft. The combinations are endless. After a few minutes swinging on a level lie, move to the back of a bunker and make a fresh line on the downslope to create a new challenge; then move to the front of the bunker and test your ability to find your line on an uphill lie. This drill will give you all the feedback you need to adjust your body angles at the setup—hip, shoulder, and spine angle—in readiness to swing either down or up the slope and find that line at impact.

The more time you spend in a bunker doing this, the better you'll get at controlling the delivery of the clubhead and hitting the sand *exactly* where you intend to. That's the secret here, which is why the line drill is one of my absolute *musts* for better sand play.#

THE SPIN SHOT

CRANK OPEN THE FACE, ZIP THE BALL

THE SHOT ALL golfers love to watch is the pop-up spinner that hops once and then stops dead, perhaps even backing up on a quicker green. To play this, I open up my stance a little more than usual, 40 degrees or so, and just widen my stance a tiny bit. This helps me get my hands lower—a tip given to me by the late, great Seve Ballesteros, who was an absolute magician with this shot, as he was with most other aspects of the short game. You want to feel physically close to the shot, ready to cut across the ball.

Thoughts on making a relatively shallow U-shaped swing will further enhance your ability to flip that open clubface beneath the ball. If you simply take your orders from the alignment of your body, you swing along the line of your toes, which automatically creates a swing path *across* the ball-to-target line. The open clubface compensates for that, and the ball floats out on a cushion of sand, straight toward the flag.

To maximize the open face and keep it open through impact, you should also experiment with your grip. Turning your hands toward each other—that is, strengthening your left and weakening the right—has the effect of really "cupping" the left wrist in the back-swing, which then helps you to keep that face wide open on the way down. Really crank that left wrist; cup it as much as you can. This is a great feeling to have on all shots around the green when you're looking to maximize loft. The more you cup your wrist, the more the club will point up to the sky in the backswing. In fact, you will find that you open the face to such an extent that no matter how hard you slice through the sand, the momentum throws the ball even higher with spin, rather than forward. Fred Couples is good at doing this—he's super strong with the left hand, super weak with the right. It really does accentuate the loft as you release the club through the sand, and it's a technique you can also apply to pitching when you need a vertical takeoff "parachute lob."

TO ACCENTUATE the open clubface, I think in terms of "cupping" my left wrist in the backswing, and then maintaining that angle all the way through impact.

RELEASE IT WITH YOUR RIGHT HAND

HERE'S ONE FOR the advanced players out there. How consistently can you play a good sand shot swinging with *just* the right hand? I love to do this, feeling the width of the swing and then allowing the clubhead to outrace the hand as I release the open clubface through the sand. When you get it just right, the results are actually better than they are with two hands on the club, and you really do learn to appreciate the sensations of impact and the way speed and clubface angle combine to produce different shots. The key to doing this consistently is giving your right elbow the freedom it needs to work away from your body and really relaxing your grip pressure, which helps you to make a consistent backswing. The more relaxed your grip is, the more impact speed you will enjoy—which is also true in the swing generally.#

PRACTICING with just your right hand on the club will reward you with the feel for the shallow, U-shaped swing that enables you to freely accelerate the open clubface through the sand—and the results can be impressive.

9-IRON

A CASE OF "THUMP AND RUN"

**VIDEO LESSON:
EXPERIMENT TO FIND
YOUR COMFORT ZONE**
Once you understand basic bunker technique, developing a variety of shots boils down to adjusting certain variables and identifying your comfort zone as you hone your natural style. Nick shows you how, with a lesson on controlling trajectory, flight, and the distance the ball rolls on the green.

ANY TIME YOU have a lot of green to work with—and this applies especially when there's a plateau to negotiate, the pin on a back tier—leave the sand wedge in the bag and reach for a 9-iron. The game plan has to change, and a less lofted club will encourage the ball to "release" with overspin so it runs more willingly toward the hole. The 9-iron was my club of choice. With practice, you'll be surprised at how much control you can achieve.

I set up in much the same way I would to play a regular sand shot, with my body open to the target line, the clubface again slightly open, but this time I put more weight on my left side. That helps me create a more V-shaped swing that chisels out a wedge of sand to pop the ball out. With its relatively narrow sole, a 9-iron does not have the same degree of bounce as a sand wedge, but opening it up just a tad makes the club workable through the sand. You're not looking for the club to dig deep down; there's a degree of bounce here as it's released. The

key is that you keep the clubhead accelerating in a short impact area—enter and exit divot in one move—so you really do need to be positive with your swing. Go down into the sand under the ball, then up and out. It's almost like a controlled "chunk." I think in terms of sticking the clubhead in the sand about an inch behind

the ball, and commit to hitting firm. The firmer you thump the sand, the farther the ball flies through the air and the more it'll run. You have to go and figure out the details with practice.

UNDERSTANDING LIES AND LIMITATIONS

DRILL

CONTROL—THAT'S THE KEY word here. If there is a secret to a polished all-around short game, it's understanding the way the ball reacts from different lies around the green and developing your clubhead awareness to such an extent that you are able to control impact. Sand shots are unique in that respect. Utilizing the bounce, the idea here is to use your sand wedge to cut a shallow divot of sand from underneath

the ball, thus propelling it into the air. Using the sand as a buffer, you literally splash it out.

The process of sizing up any bunker shot begins the moment you step into the sand. Through your feet, you'll be able to determine the quality of the surface, the texture, and the depth of the sand you have to work with. In soft, powdery sand, the clubhead will naturally want to dig more deeply. To guard against this, you have to adjust your setup position to make a shallow U-shaped swing. Instinctively, you must learn to spread your weight evenly between your feet, and lay the clubface wide open to maximize the effect of the bounce.

By contrast, on firm or wet sand, it's your job to make the club dig underneath the ball. The wide sole that characterizes a sand wedge will resist doing this, which is why it's a good idea in this situation to experiment with a gap (52 to 56 degrees) or regular pitching wedge. Your setup this time must be designed to produce a sharper, V-shaped swing. Shift the majority of your weight onto your left side and play these shots with a square clubface. Impact needs to be down and then level for a split second to avoid the bounce kicking up the clubhead.

Tied to the quality of sand, the way your ball is lying in the bunker is another key factor in determining what you can realistically achieve. The depth of sand you have to take to get the clubface fully underneath the ball determines the amount of spin, if any, that you're able to create. No matter how skilled you are, different lies will yield different reactions.

Early in my career, I was fortunate to watch the great Gary Player put on a bunker clinic in which he used a simple drill to illustrate what you should expect to achieve out of different lies. I've used it ever since, and it can offer you no better way to read sand and gauge how the ball will react. It works like this: Arrange four balls in a line, each time making the lie slightly worse than the one before it, a perfectly "clean" lie to a plugged ball. Then put the same swing on each one and see what you get.

How far does each shot carry onto the green? How much does the ball run?

First, the clean lie. No problems here—you can play a regular splash shot with a wide-open clubface and create a decent amount of backspin. With the ball in a slight depression, I'd again use an open clubface and play the exact same shot, only this time I'd expect a slightly lower ball-flight, and the shot would run a little farther on the green. The third ball in your line, semi-plugged, will come out lower and run farther still, while the fully plugged ball needs a good thump to pop it out, and will run the farthest.

The beauty of a drill like this is that you can use it to experiment with the variables you can control and use the feedback to understand the effect this has on the way each shot unfolds. Say, for example, you decide to play them all with your most lofted wedge, and lay the clubface wide open. What combination of flight and roll do you get

VIDEO LESSON:
A TIP FROM GARY PLAYER
Recalling a classic practice drill that has stood the test of time, Nick illustrates the way in which the lie of the ball in the sand will always dictate what you are able to achieve in escaping a greenside bunker.

on each of these four shots? What happens if you play them all again, but this time with a lazier, almost slow-motion type of swing? The results will be different, and with each combination of lie, swing type, and clubface angle, you'll be learning something new about your ability to control the golf ball from a specific situation.#

PLUGGED?

STICK THE CLUBHEAD IN THE SAND

THERE'S NOTHING worse than misjudging your approach and finding your ball plugged in its own pitch mark. But don't think you have to create a sandstorm to get the ball out. There's a more subtle and effective way. The angle of the clubface combined with the angle of attack is the key. When your ball is partially submerged, you need to encourage the clubface to dig in order to take the necessary divot of sand. To do that, you square up the leading edge, thus diminishing the bounce effect.

Let's assume the ball is semi-plugged in soft sand. To play this shot, I would take a fairly open

stance, move the ball back of center, and settle most of my weight onto my left side. I then open the clubface just a fraction and focus on making a fairly steep V-shaped swing with noticeable wrist break. Aiming to strike a couple of inches behind the ball, I thump the sand and leave the clubhead in there, compressing the sand under the ball and thus creating the force that pops it out. If you set aside some time to practice this shot, I think you might be surprised at how much control you can exert over the ball. It all hinges on feel. The farther you want the ball to run, the

more you square the face and the harder you thump the sand.

In the extreme case of a fully plugged ball, it's worth experimenting with a slightly closed clubface, and you should also consider the option of taking your thinnest soled wedge, which helps to eliminate the bounce factor altogether and assists you in digging beneath the ball.

Trust the physics involved. Lean into the shot, keeping your right shoulder as high as possible, and then set the club up as quickly and fully as you can, swinging outside your target line, before thumping it down into the sand. As long as the clubhead is going down, the ball will pop up and out of the bunker. It's impossible to create any backspin, so make sure you allow for a significant amount of run when you visualize the shot.

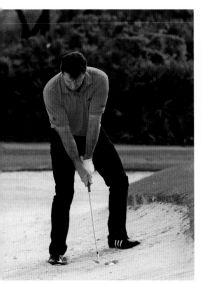

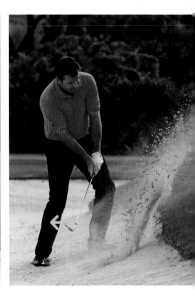

EXTREME SPORT?
TRY THE INSTANT RECOIL

SOME OF THE recoveries we see on tour these days are remarkable, and one little trick that I've picked up features a dramatic recoiling of the clubhead a split second after imact—it's almost as if the clubhead bounces back out of the sand. This technique is useful whenever you find a ball fully plugged in the face of a bunker. Ordinarily you'd get yourself into a position to give it a hefty thump with a relatively square clubface and little to no follow-through to speak of, resigned to the fact that your fate is up in the air somewhat (as indeed you hope the ball will be). Other than the precise speed at which you thump the sand, there's no real control here. A good result is getting the ball safely out and onto the green.

But there's another solution, and apart from anything else, it's a lot of fun. The "recoil" shot does exactly what it says on the label: Using a square to slightly closed clubface, commit to whacking the sand two inches behind the ball, and pull the clubhead out again almost at the moment you make contact. *Doiiing!* The key to pulling this shot off is the timing. If you tell yourself to pull the clubhead out just as it makes contact, by the time you actually *do* pull it back, the clubhead will have exploded into the sand and then recoiled sharply back out. What's happening is, if you stop your arms, your wrists and the clubhead keep going, really compressing the sand up and out. When you get this right, the controlled explosion releases just enough sand to pop the ball up and out of the bunker, and you'll be amazed at the control you can achieve. Even from a fully plugged lie, you can actually have the ball come up quite softly and roll just a matter of feet on the green. You live and learn.

DOWNSLOPE
"CHASE" THE CLUBHEAD AFTER THE BALL

THE DOWNHILL LIE is the toughest of all greenside trap shots—simply getting the ball out and onto the green is a result in itself. Even the most skillful player is resigned to the fact that the downslope effectively diminishes the loft of the sand wedge and that the ball is going to come out low with very little in the way of backspin, so factor in a significant element of run. But again, with a little practice, you don't need to fear these shots. You simply need to understand how to play them.

On any sort of slope, your thoughts must be geared toward neutralizing the angles, leaving you in a position to make as regular a swing as possible. That involves setting your spine as perpendicular to the slope as you can get it, which in this case involves placing significantly more weight on your foot that's set lower as you marry up your hip and shoulder angles to the run of the ground, or at least as close to parallel as comfortable. Grip down, too. Not only does this help activate your wrist action, but it shortens the length of the shaft, which gives you a little extra clearance to avoid striking the sand or the lip of the bunker as you make your backswing.

The role of the lower body is now even more important than ever. Flex your knees to provide a real suspension unit—create a balance that feels stable, capable

NEVER TRY to lean back and scoop it up. It's the open face and extra clubhead speed that get it airborne.

of supporting the rotation of your upper body. Much depends on the texture of the sand, but generally speaking, you don't expect to find much depth of sand in the back of a trap, and you don't want to encourage bounce. I would open the clubface only marginally before rehearsing the initial backswing motion a couple of times—a sand-shot waggle to keep the wrists alive to the job they have to do. Remember, the Rules of Golf do not permit touching the sand, so be careful as you rehearse the initial few feet of your backswing. On a severe downslope, you will need a fairly pronounced wrist action to avoid touching the sand or colliding with the back lip of the bunker. To be on the safe side, exaggerate your wrist action. As you crank those wrists up, visual-

ize chasing the clubhead down. Move your right shoulder down and through even if it pulls you forward and a little off-balance. Finishing with all your weight on your left foot is a good thing.

This is no easy assignment, and you're going to have to practice regularly to gain the confidence necessary to release the right hand and really throw the club-

head down the slope. I encourage hitting balls off a downhill lie as a terrific exercise for all golfers to feel the way in which you need to speed up your downward arm action and release the right hand to enjoy the ball-turf strike that characterizes good iron play. And the better your iron play, the less you'll have to worry about finding your ball in a position like this.

UPSLOPE

YOU HAVE TO BE AGGRESSIVE

THE UPHILL LIE is a much easier proposition. Given that even the slightest upslope adds loft to whatever club you're using, getting the ball up in the air isn't a problem. Depending on the severity of the lie, getting it to move *forward* is usually the greater challenge.

On a relatively gentle incline, you can adopt the same approach we took with the downhill shot: Think in terms of neutralizing the slope with your setup position. That involves leaning your spine to the right until you're in a position to make a fairly level swing *up* the slope. Your right side absorbs most of your weight while your feet and knees are fine-tuned shock absorbers providing the feedback that enables you to establish and maintain a balanced position. Once you have that surety of footing, the flexed right knee and thigh remain solid, providing you with a resistance to turn against as you make your backswing.

You'll learn to read the sand and the severity of the slope to determine whether you need to open the clubface at all, but as a general rule, that's not necessary. In fact, your sand wedge is not the automatic choice, either. You have to judge each shot on its merits, but be prepared to experiment with any one of your wedges. On a severe upslope, a regular pitching wedge may be a smarter proposi-

tion. You have some margin for error here; whether you hit one, two, or three inches behind the ball, it will come out in an explosion of sand. But the better you get at hitting just an inch behind it, the more control you'll have over landing distance. The momentum is upward, rather than forward, so commit yourself to swinging hard *into* the slope.

Faced with a particularly steep uphill lie, I'll sometimes think in terms of collapsing my left arm as I release the clubhead so that I effectively pull it up and through the sand. In other words, I thump the sand and then haul the clubface up the slope. In the through-swing, my hands work around toward my left shoulder, and in so doing help the ball out. Just another idea for you to go out and try.

INTERMEDIATE SHOTS
HOW TO REGULATE DISTANCE

SAND SHOTS GET tougher the farther you are from the green. Those from intermediate range—say, 30 to 60 yards from the pin—are perhaps the toughest of all. A regular greenside bunker shot gives you a reasonable margin for error. You can hit the sand one, two, or three inches behind the ball and still get a decent result. There's no such luxury here. It's all about precision. And it's a shot even tour players find difficult.

I always worked the theory that you should take a consistent cut of sand—this time aiming no more than an inch behind to right into the back of the ball—and regulate distance with the length of your swing and subsequent acceleration through impact. I set up to these shots much as I would a wedge from the fairway, "cheating" impact with my body slightly open to the target and my weight evenly spread between my feet. The one difference is that the

ball is now back of center in my stance, and the clubface is square to the target.

As I choke down on the grip, my thoughts are based on the trusted "set-and-rotate" philosophy, which helps produce a compact back-swing and a relatively shallow downswing. The actual distance of the shot dictates the speed of the swing and the acceleration through impact. On a 40-yard shot with a 53-degree wedge, I'd be looking to repeat a regular three-quarter swing with a balanced three-quarter finish. A 60-yard shot would require a fuller swing and a fuller finish. It's up to you to establish your optimal range.

As you gradually increase your landing distance with each of

your wedges, you'll eventually get to a point where it stops being an explosion and becomes a pure strike. Rather than hit the sand, you're now trying to strike the ball first. There's a transition to be discovered. I know, for example, that a full explosion shot with a 53-degree wedge (that is, hitting the sand an inch behind the ball) gives me a shot of around 60 yards. After that, I'm looking for a pure, clean strike, which will give me a shot of up to 100 yards, depending on my speed and tempo. A full, clean strike with a 60-degree wedge gives me 70-plus yards. Again, you must identify your "best" yardages with your chosen wedges.

To take the ball cleanly, I suggest that you move it farther back in your stance—an inch or so back of center—and focus on trapping it off the surface with a swing built on rhythm and balance. Above all, try to keep your body "centered." Push your knees out, to firm them up, and then use them as shock absorbers as you turn your trunk back and through. The key is to keep your lower body very passive and let your arms and shoulders do all the work. On a specific point, I find that strengthening my left-hand grip helps to guard against picking the club up too steeply in the backswing, which is always a danger when you play the ball back in the stance. Turning the left hand slightly to the right of

a normal position encourages you to rotate your left forearm correctly away from the ball, thus setting up a good angle of attack in the downswing.

The more practice and research you do here, the more valuable information you will have at your fingertips out on the course. Just as we explored in Chapter 8, your pitching clubs promise a matrix of controlled yardages, with the Clockface Principle as good a means as any for developing your scoring system. As you improve your consistency of strike on these sand shots, you can use that same formula here to register your "best" distances (not forgetting your 9-iron—which can often prove a valuable option).

FAIRWAY BUNKER SHOTS
A TRUE TEST OF PRECISION

MY ADVICE? BE rational, not reckless. Before choosing the appropriate club, you need to assess the shot that faces you. Step into the bunker and take a good look at how the ball is lying. As you do this, you will get some idea of the texture of the sand through the soles of your shoes—and that's valuable information. Just be aware that the Rules of Golf do not allow you to "test" the sand prior to playing a shot; shuffling your feet in a bid to gauge the depth of the sand around your ball, for example, would incur a penalty.

If the lie is poor, your decision is made for you: Play safe. Where would you most like to be playing your *next* shot from? Determine a safety zone, and then plot the easiest route back to the fairway. Always err on the side of caution—and if in doubt, take the more lofted club.

Looking on the brighter side, if the lie is good and the possibility of playing a full shot exists, how far do you have to fly the ball? Will the club that you need to cover that distance give you the trajectory to clear the front lip? These are the questions that need to be answered.

Say you have 160 yards to go. From the fairway, that might ordinarily suggest a 7- or 8-iron, depending on conditions. Out of the bunker, I would take an extra club and grip down the shaft half an inch or so. With the more powerful loft, you can swing comfortably within your ability and still achieve the desired yardage.

Picking the ball cleanly before the club strikes the sand is the key to the success of these shots, and to achieve that, I advise playing the ball from the middle of the stance and with your weight evenly spread between your feet. Once I'm in position at the setup, my thoughts then turn toward making a silky-smooth swing, the entire motion controlled by the torso and the arms. Precision is key. As soon as you force a shot like this, you're liable to lose your footing and place the strike in jeopardy.

As we discussed in Chapter 4, "Timing and Tempo," hitting balls from a fairway bunker is one of the best tests there is for the quality of your swing motion and balance. And let me share a little secret here: When I practice these shots, I always think about keeping the right shoulder high at the setup. A good way to achieve this is to reverse the position of your hands on the grip as you get yourself into position—that is, placing the left hand below the right as you set up to the ball. This has the desired effect of leveling the shoulders. Once you're comfortable, revert to your normal grip but keep that right shoulder in this higher position. During the swing this will assist you in taking the ball cleanly. I also like to have the feeling of moving my body ever so slightly toward the target in the downswing. This helps me keep my hands ahead of the clubface and meet the ball cleanly (slightly "thin" is better than fat). In other words, with what amounts to a slight sway, I simply ease myself into the shot. My eyes are fixed on the back of the ball—the old trick of focusing on a specific dimple works wonders here—and I keep my footwork to a minimum as I unwind and accelerate to a full and balanced finish.

1996 *A moment of contemplation at the par-5 13th hole at Augusta National during the final round of the Masters.*

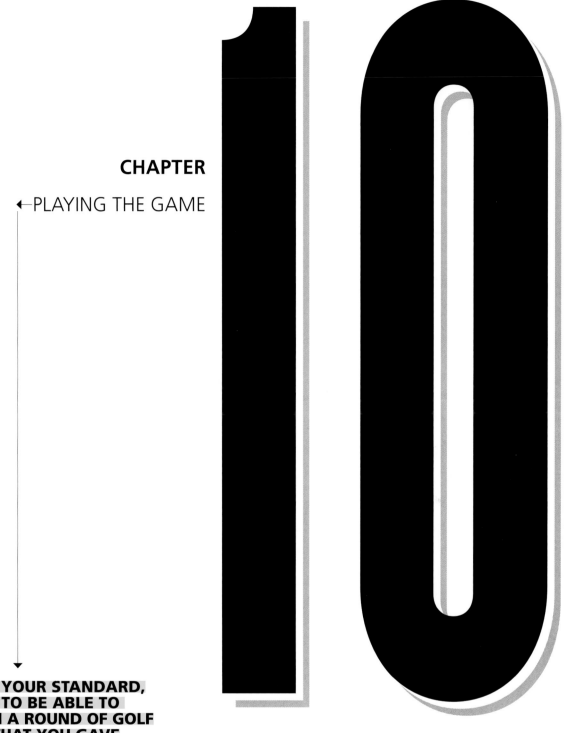

CHAPTER

←PLAYING THE GAME

WHATEVER YOUR STANDARD,
YOU WANT TO BE ABLE TO
REFLECT ON A ROUND OF GOLF
SATISFIED THAT YOU GAVE
100 PERCENT—NOT ONLY TO
THE TASK OF PHYSICALLY STRIKING
THE BALL, BUT APPLYING YOUR
THOUGHTS AND FOCUS TO THE
ART OF PLAYING THE GAME.

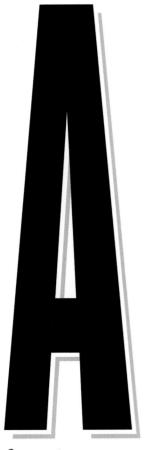

AFTER A PLAYING career spanning over 30 years—and one timed perfectly to coincide with what many would agree was a golden era in the history of the professional game—I had no complaints retiring from the circuit in 2005 and focusing my attention on other interests, not least of which is my television work for CBS Sports and Golf Channel. I had a pretty decent run, all told, and I was fortunate enough to have played with, and competed alongside, many of the greatest players the game has ever seen—Jack Nicklaus, Tom Watson, Nick Price, Greg Norman, Tiger Woods, and Severiano Ballesteros among them. Those memories will certainly last me a lifetime.

But the world moves on, and golf has moved with it. During my travels around the globe promoting the Faldo Series, a junior initiative that each year attracts over 7,000 young players in 30-plus countries, I've marveled at the depth of talent that exists in a new generation of golfers who have grown up with the incredible knowledge and technology that define the game today. It has been my privilege to have played golf and designed courses all over the world, and to witness what can only be described as an explosion in the game, the evidence of which we are seeing regularly on leaderboards here on the PGA Tour and indeed across all of the professional tours.

In my day job for television, I like to run through the draw sheet at the start of a week and highlight the names of the players who, if they are on their game, have a chance of winning. Back in my era, that might have been half a dozen serious contenders at a major; these days, I regularly have 40 names underlined, each one a potential champion. Such is the depth in the game at the highest level today.

The upshot, of course, is that winning is getting harder. Wherever you stand on the "Great Equipment Debate," there is no denying the fact that modern technology has all but wiped out the advantage once enjoyed by the superior ball-striker, and the game

has become an even tougher examination of short-game and putting skills. And the ability to *score* is quite distinct from the ability to strike a golf ball. I see many young players who are impressive on the range or in the early rounds of a tournament, where there is no real pressure on their swing. The real test, of course, is how well you hit the ball as the pressure of winning or performing well increases, which boils down to how well you manage your game and your emotions. Now the competitive instinct is challenged, which is why self-control, self-belief, and mental toughness largely determine success.

The players who consistently make the grade are the players who take in their stride all the unpredictable bounces and difficult lies—all the shots that test or push their abilities beyond their comfort level. These are the players who relish the art of scrambling when they miss a fairway or a green. It's the same at club level. There is always someone who stands out, a player who has that something extra special, whether it's the feel in his hands or a stomach for pressure, the guts to make something happen. Or simply a player who knows how to practice and prepare for the challenges that lie in store when it comes to *playing the game.*

Balance in all things is positive. And you learn as you get older. I know now, for example, that I

PLAYING TO THE PICTURE:
I played my best golf when my swing thoughts were directed toward my goal, my target—as they were at Augusta in 1996.

used to spend too much of my time thinking about the construction of my backswing—that is, what was going on *behind* the ball—and not enough on what was going to happen through the ball and toward the target. When I reflect on my career, I realize that I always played my best golf when my thoughts were going *that* way: toward the target. In full flow, my final rounds at many of the major championships I contested have been examples of this—all I concentrated on was my follow-through, changing the shape of my through-swing to influence the flight of the ball. Engaging the target became my overriding priority in the hour or so that I would spend warming up before a tournament round, and I want this to be your priority, too. Working on the mechanics

of your swing is all well and good between games, and the earlier chapters of the book provide you with all the theory you need to do that effectively and build a solid technique. But when it comes to preparing yourself for a round of golf, to play for real, the only thing you should be thinking about is harnessing your energy and channeling it toward a specific target, fashioning your swing to suit the shape of shot you're looking for. That is what good golf is all about.

You get out of this game only what you're prepared to put into it. That philosophy is also true in life, and I firmly believe in it. Whatever your personal goals may be—to win the club championship, shoot your first score under 100, or break that magical figure of 70 for the first time—you need determination to make the breakthrough. If you're willing to work at your game and consider all of the variables that make it such a great voyage of discovery, who knows? Here are a few ideas to ponder.

WORK ON POSITIVE PICTURES, BUILD GOOD HABITS . . .

ASSUMING YOU really do want to give yourself the best possible chance of playing well, I suggest finding a little time before heading to the range to sit down quietly in the locker room and contemplate the day ahead. Do some basic breathing exercises and relax. Chances are you were tearing all over the place before arriving at the club, so take this time to leave behind the stresses and strains of everyday life and concentrate on the depth and rhythm of your breathing and get yourself on an even keel. (It is said that Ben Hogan made it his policy to drive to the course well under the speed limit to help prepare for the day. To me, that creates a wonderful image of calmness, and it's one you should keep in mind.)

As you do this, think about your objectives for the round. What do you want to achieve? That will create a set of pictures in your mind. You may see (and indeed fear!) a few tough shots out there, particularly on potential "bogey holes," which is fine. These are precisely the mental hurdles we all have to overcome. But wouldn't it be nice to see yourself walking off the 18th green having played the best round of your life? Ask yourself how you might achieve that. Think it through. Most golfers get stuck in a rut because they never change their pictures, their habits, or the way they perceive their own game. If there's a hole that always seems to cause you trouble, change your game plan and see yourself hitting the shots that will help you negotiate it. Say, for example, there's a tight par 4 with trees all down the right-hand side, and you habitually hit driver and carve it into the thick of them. Most likely, that's the picture you see long before you get there. Change that picture. And the club. If you can't handle a driver on that particular hole, change to something different, a club you *know* you can trust to hit the ball where you want to hit it. Change your strategy. Paint fresh new images in your mind.

On the range before your round, the key is to first get your "engine" running, to develop some feel in the hands and arms, and then to reinforce these positive images with target-oriented practice. To kick things off, spend a couple of minutes stretching your muscles with a few golf-specific exercises designed to help you make a better swing. Starting with the wrists, forearms, and shoulders, I do some stretch and resistance work, holding this "loaded" position for a few seconds and then repeating it (on both sides). Scientific research has revealed to us the vital role of the ankles in facilitating the chain reaction of motion from the ground up—through the feet, the legs, the hips, and into the torso. If your ankles are "tight," you lose that dynamism. So try to combine some basic stretching to focus on this interaction you have with the ground, perhaps rocking back and forth from heel to toe in posture to warm up the ankles. Then move on the pivot motion itself, waking up the muscles in the trunk—the all-important abdominals that are instrumental in generating "core" rotation and speed.

HARNESS THE POWER OF THE MIND AND BODY: Warming up on the range provides the opportunity to stretch key muscles in readiness to make a good swing. Spend a few minutes rehearsing your motion with your eyes closed—that will help you to identify the source of your natural tempo.

I've always found that swinging a club with just the right hand is an effective exercise here, and as you do this, remember the importance of allowing the right elbow its freedom as you create width and *complete* your backswing. For me, the most important thing is to sense that the shoulders are doing all of the work. Thanks to a good coiling motion of the upper body, the big muscles provide the structure of a solid swing.

To complete your basic warm-up, try swinging a club with your eyes closed (as we first looked at in Chapter 4). This is something I've always included in my warm-up routine because it's one of the best exercises I know to get myself in tune with my swing on any given day. I find that I'm made aware of the hinging and "setting" of the wrists as I make my backswing turn, and then especially on the moments through the impact area as I swing to a finish. The key is to start slowly and gradually build your speed and momentum. And always hold your finish for several seconds with your body turned fully through to face the target, which

is great for balance awareness. Allow the sensations to soak in. If there's a patch of rough near the first tee, make a few full swings in there and feel the resistance of the grass as you accelerate the club through to that finish. That's a great way to focus your awareness on generating speed where it matters most.

REMEMBER: FROM the moment you set up to the ball, *balance = power*. There are many parallels in other sports and disciplines: Tennis players talk about hav-

ing their weight forward and the importance of "moving into the shot." Boxers throw their hardest punches with their weight on the balls of their feet (not sitting back on their heels). It's proven in martial arts that the weight has to be forward to maximize the potential of harnessing the power within and to generate speed. I even learned recently that opera singers have to tip their weight

slightly toward the balls of their feet to execute their breathing technique. It's all about projection. We're gearing ourselves up to project our momentum, our energy, in the direction of the target. And there is just no escaping the importance of a good *athletic* posture. Which is why I keep coming back to my No. 1 MUST—*knees.* The next time you're out hitting balls, do this simple test: Take your stance, lift your heels until you feel your weight supported on the balls of the feet, then flex your knees to settle into posture. This routine immediately braces the legs and creates just the right amount of tension in the thighs and backside to stabilize the swing—exactly the reminder you need before you go out to play. The test I always give to myself then is

to keep my knees nice and solid as I make my backswing, turning my left shoulder under my chin before unwinding through to the target. The key is that the right knee *resists* the rotation of the hips and upper body in the backswing—but it must never lock up. That right knee support is vital at every level of skill. And that's as technical as it gets in a warm-up session. With your swing ticking over, your focus now has to be on repeating a good rhythm and engaging your *target.*

T AKING YOUR GAME from the range to the first tee is one of the toughest things for many players, but it can be made a lot easier if you align

your thought process as closely as possible with the challenges you face on the course itself. Let me give you an example with one of my favorite practice routines that became something of a tradition at Augusta during Masters week. Having warmed up through the set, hitting a handful of balls with each club, I then turned my thoughts to my game plan. I would imagine that I was standing on the first tee and try to picture the shape of the drive in my mind. For me, this hole sets up nicely for a fade aimed at the left half of the fairway. I would then go through my pre-shot routine—and that includes a proper full rehearsal with a practice swing—and then hit my opening tee shot. Watching the flight of the ball, I was able to determine pretty well where my drive would have finished and calculate what I had left to the green. Scanning the yardage book, my caddie, Fanny Sunneson, would give me the detailed information—the yardage, hole location, wind direction, etc.—and I would then apply the same set of rules to the second shot: Pick a shot, "see" it, feel it (with a rehearsal swing), and then commit to it (action). And so it goes on. In a short space of time, you could actually play a whole round of golf like this,

or at least the opening few holes and some of the key shots on the front nine. The key is that you go through the motions exactly as you would on the golf course. That's the trick to staying focused and making your practice session more productive and meaningful.

Clearly, this sort of exercise checks all the boxes when it comes to *practicing with a purpose*. Not only are you running through the process of physically hitting the shots, but you are reading the game and tuning mind and body, which in the long run will help you to cope with pressure when it comes to hitting real shots out on the course. The more you rehearse this visualization technique, the more you'll learn about the way your swing holds up under the gun. Call the shot, and then challenge yourself to hit it. How close did you get to the picture in your mind? If there's a "bogey hole" that you fear, now is the time to re-create that hole in your mind and plan a new way of dealing with it. The key is to replace the negatives with more positive thoughts. A great deal has been written about the mental side of the game, and much of it makes a lot of sense. But, equally, there is a tendency to make too much of what is really quite a simple matter. You have to be honest with yourself and appraise your game. I like Sam Snead's philosophy: *If you're nervous about hitting a 7-iron, go practice your 7-iron!*

PLAY "TOURNAMENT LIES"

I **ALWAYS LOVED TO** spend time around a practice green working on different types of shots, experimenting with various wedges and really getting a feel for spin and trajectory. Practicing the short-game skills is your passport to lower scoring. But don't just keep on rolling each ball onto a perfect lie—if you want to be fully prepared for what you'll experience on the course, you have to be more creative than that. You have to make your practice realistic. "Okay, give me some tournament lies," I'd say to my caddie. That was Fanny's cue to take a basket of balls and scatter them, giving me the challenge of playing each ball "as it lies," doing my best to conjure a shot that would get close to the pin. If there was a decent patch of rough around a bunker, I'd experiment to discover what I could expect to do with a certain type of shot, studying how each ball flies and gauging its reaction on the green. This is a drill that helps you develop that versatility—have some fun with it.#

TRY MY DE-LOFT EXERCISE FOR A MORE POSITIVE STRIKE

T **HE SECRET TO** making good contact on all of your wedge shots around the green is to commit 100 percent to a positive acceleration in the downswing so that your hands lead the clubhead through the ball. The one thing you must *never* do is try to help a wedge shot up into the air with a "scoop" or a flick at the ball with the right hand. One way to develop the technique that will reward you with a more solid and consistent strike is to imagine taking a couple of degrees off the natural loft of the clubface as you return it to the back of the ball. So, for example, if you are using a 60-degree wedge, say to yourself "60 degrees" at address, and then "58" as you accelerate smoothly toward impact. Thoughts of de-lofting the clubface encourage the softness in the wrists that is vital as you transition from backswing to downswing, that gentle "lag" in the stroke further helping you to accelerate down into the ball for crisp contact.#

TAKE A HALF-SET, TEST YOUR IMAGINATION . . .

THE LEARNING CURVE:
With just a handful of clubs, you have no option but to improvise and manufacture shots.

THE DAY AFTER winning The Open at Muirfield in 1992, I played a friendly game at Swinley Forest, a wonderful Harry Colt heathland course in Berkshire, on the outskirts of London. The old caddie who greeted me at the clubhouse was lost for words when I handed him a small pencil bag that contained just a half-set of clubs: driver, 2-iron, 5-iron, 8-iron, wedge, and putter. I thoroughly enjoyed my round and shot 65.

More than anything, playing with just a handful of clubs teaches you the art of manufacturing shots and judging distance. Where you might normally expect to play a 6-iron but don't have one, you're forced to play a quiet 5, or rake in a hard 7. I've always relished this sort of practice simply because it makes you stop and *think*. The trick is to get as sharp a visual as you can in your mind of the shot that fits the picture, and then give yourself one go at pulling it off. That's the key to staying competitive, both mentally and physically. Play in the early morning or late in the evening, when the course is quiet. When you're alone with your thoughts, you can nominate a cut-up shot one minute, then punch the ball the next. Bend shots around trees, make the ball turn both ways.

Another good exercise—and particularly if you tend to play most of your golf on one course—is to go out and limit yourself to hitting a hybrid or a long iron off the tee, so that you create a whole new set of approach shots at par 4s. So many amateurs get stale playing their regular course, automatically pulling a club on the tee before actually looking at the hole

VIDEO LESSON: CONSISTENCY THROUGH THE BAG
Whatever your level, a good strategy revolves around distance control and consistency of ball-striking. The Track-Man "combined test" enables you to pinpoint your strengths and weaknesses all the way through the bag.

or giving a thought to the yardage and playing conditions. We get into routines and habits that are tough to break, and yet you have to break them if you want to see improvement. Where you would blast away on a par 5, knowing full well you cannot reach the green in two shots, aim for a layup to your favorite number for the wedge shot in.

Playing a few holes on your own will also give you the opportunity to try a simple experiment. On a typical par 4, tee up a ball as close as you can to the left-hand marker. Set up to the ball and take a look down the fairway. Then tee another as close as possible to the right-hand marker and compare the views.

If you play with a natural fade, as I do, you'll feel more comfortable playing from the *right* side of the tee. That suits your shape, and offers you the most inviting view of the fairway. It maximizes your target area. If you draw the ball, the left side of the tee is where you'll feel most comfortable. And remember: There is nothing in the rules to prevent you from standing *outside* the teeing area, as long as your ball is teed up between the markers.

The process of "targeting" shots clearly in your mind has to become an integral part of your pre-shot routine. Whatever your favored shot, don't stand on the tee and consider the entire width

of the fairway your target area. Not only is this much too vague, it opens the door for complacency. Unless you have a specific target against which to measure your performance off the tee, you can never hope to be consistent. The key is to sharpen your focus with "tunnel vision." Allowing for your shape, take dead aim on some specific target or object, perhaps a tree or a distant rooftop, anything that enables you to pinpoint your alignment. Give yourself a margin for error. With a driver, I usually stand behind the ball and picture a circle in the fairway, about 10 yards across. That's a comfortable and realistic safety zone.

Here's something else to consider. The Rules of Golf allow you to tee your ball up to a maximum of two club-lengths *behind* the line of the tee markers. That gives you some leeway to play with, which can be particularly useful when you get an in-between yardage on a par 3. Let's assume a hole measures 170 yards. For me, a good 6-iron flies around 175 yards, and in this example, the pin is out of range with a 7. The solution? If I tee the ball back by the two yards I am allowed, that will often make the difference between hitting it "easy" and hitting a full shot.

HYBRID TO THE RESCUE!

CATCH IT FLUSH, and there's not a more satisfying shot in golf than a rifled long iron. But they are tough to hit, even for pros who work on their swing every day. One of the most noticeable trends on tour over the last 10 years has been the decline of the 1-, 2-, and even 3-iron in favor of the modern hybrid. With a relatively small head, shallow face, and low center of gravity, these clubs have become the friendliest and most versatile in the bag. With a little practice, you can enjoy playing a knockdown "stinger" off the tee, floating a high, soft-landing approach shot from the fairway, and pulling off spectacular escape shots from a bunker or off a poor lie. Hybrids also provide a useful "chip-putt" solution just around the fringe of the green.

My thought process with a hybrid out of a fairway bunker is the same as it would be with a long iron. I try to stand tall at address, and a good waggle programs the sensation of the wrist-and-forearm rotation I'm looking for. My feet and knees remain very passive (because of the nature of your footing, the lower body tends not to be as active as it would be from the fairway), and I tell myself to swing easy, with perhaps 80 percent effort. I also grip down the club half an inch, and I like to have a sense of my arms being nicely stretched out as I hover the clubhead behind the ball. The key then is to focus your eyes precisely on the back of the ball, and to keep your head still as you "collect" it cleanly through impact and dispatch the shot with the perfect trajectory as the clubhead does its job.

Clearly, the one danger here in the sand is catching the shot fat. To avoid that, think in terms of getting the back of your left hand to the ball *before* the clubhead. In other words, feel that you "hold off" the release ever so slightly; that way you'll catch the ball cleanly. If I need to add loft to hit the ball higher, I increase the rotation of my left forearm and the "cupping" in my left wrist as I turn my upper body and wind up the backswing, or simply open the clubface a fraction and aim left, picturing a high fade.

FOCUS ON THE QUALITY OF THE STRIKE

WHEN I LOOK back on various stages in the evolution of my golf swing, I see that there are times when I may have gone too far with the rotation of the left wrist and the forearms in the early stages of the backswing. Certainly in that black-and-white sequence taken on the range at Muirfield in 1987, when I was fresh from rebuilding my swing with David Leadbetter, there are signs of a little too much rotation. Through the years, as I learned to use my body more effectively, I preferred to see this "cupping" of the wrists in the backswing; to me, this is a little easier on the hands and arms. Fast-forward to the latter stages of my career, and this was definitely the feeling I looked for at Augusta in 1996, quite a departure from my rotation-dominated swing of the late 1980s. That's one of the fascinating things about this game— things do change as you get older.

Whether or not this cupping was Hogan's secret, who knows.

I was once told it was, along with the way he *fired* the right knee. Perhaps it was a package deal—when you set the club up with that cupping in the left wrist, you're then able to fire the right side and hold on to the angle of the clubface as you release it through the play zone. You need strength to do this, but it's a great feeling. Having that confidence in the position of the clubface was always one of my greatest assets. In fact, I'd often practice with my attention 100 percent focused on the clubface angle in relation to my hands and forearms. We talk about having our attention on the knees or the hips or shoulders, but try it with your attention solely on the clubface. Try it hitting balls. How accurately can you feel that clubface and return it exactly where you want the ball to go?

Whenever I worked on shaping shots, I used to picture a little piece of sandpaper on the middle of the clubface. I'd see it directly behind the ball at setup. Then I'd simply imagine ripping that piece of sandpaper across the ball to impart whatever spin I was looking for. *Swoosh* through impact, feeling and hearing the spin on the ball. What I'm trying to stress here is that it's so important to think about the nature of the strike you're looking to achieve. Playing to that picture again. That's a nice visual image to have in mind that gets you thinking along the right lines for strike, spin, and control.

A lot of people talk about "quiet hands" in a good golf swing. I don't agree with that at all. One of the illustrations I always liked was that famous Anthony Ravielli drawing of Ben Hogan at the start of *The Modern Fundamentals of Golf,* with the motor inside his torso and electric wires running through his arms and into the hands. That's where the sparks are—the lightning is in the hands. All good players have the ability to save the shot with good hand action, with that extra sense of *feel.* As I've said many times, the more reliable your body action, the more you can enjoy playing golf with the forearms and hands, transferring the thoughts and visuals in your head to the flight of the ball. Practice and experience give you that ability to slow it all down and take as much as

400 rpm off the ball; or add a little more hand action, "trap" the ball a little more sharply, and increase backspin.

When I look around the game today, I'd say that using the body correctly—and by that I mean creating good posture angles and then *completing* the turn, the rotation, on either side of the ball—is the most obvious common denominator among the fit and strong young players who enjoy the "power game" afforded by modern equipment. The athleticism is in the body action, while the way the arms work in relation to the body determines your natural shape of shot, whether that's left-to-right or right-to-left. We all have a tendency, one way or the other. And the most successful players never fight it.

COME RAIN OR SHINE...

MEMBERS AT Welwyn Garden City used to think I was mad when I would stand on the range hitting balls in the wind and rain. But you have to be prepared for all conditions, and that includes swinging the club with a set of waterproofs on. These days, performance outerwear is so incredibly lightweight and flexible that you hardly know you're wearing it, but there is a certain mind-set you have to be familiar with in poor weather conditions. Think about what you have to do to give yourself the best chance of hitting a good shot in wind and rain. *Club up and swing easy with "soft arms"*—that's a wet-weather *must*. Remember, the ball isn't going to run very far, so you have to carry it to your target distance. As a further precaution against catching the shot "heavy," I would also grip down half an inch or so—which again has to be factored in to your club selection.

Here are a few more common-sense ideas on playing wet-weather golf:

→ Pack at least two dry towels in your golf bag.

→ If you wear a glove, carry two or three spares, preferably in a ziplock polyethylene bag. Better still, get yourself a wet-weather glove—the latest versions offer incredible traction no matter how wet they get.

→ Be extra careful around the green. Surface water can accumulate quickly, so check your route to the hole before playing any type of running shot. Where ordinarily you might choose to chip the ball, you might find the aerial route is the better option.

→ In the sand, square up the clubface. When you face a greenside bunker shot and the sand is wet and firm, your sand wedge won't "bounce" as willingly as it would in dry conditions. You must encourage the leading edge to dig, so set up with the clubface relatively square.

→ Play for less break on putts. On a wet surface, the ball won't take the break as much as it does on dry, quick greens.

**VIDEO LESSON:
FORWARD THINKING**

Why the quality of your
follow-through is the key
to finding your target.

AUGUSTA NATIONAL: 12th HOLE

The 12th at Augusta National, "Golden Bell," may be one of the prettiest and most photographed short holes in golf; it also happens to be one of the most treacherous. In the space of just 155 yards, this is a hole that encapsulates Dr. Alister MacKenzie's brilliance as an architect, the slender green no more than nine yards deep at the waist, and the silent waters of Rae's Creek lurking in the foreground. Standing on the tee, the player has a decision to make: Due to the angle at which the green is set, you are effectively looking at three distinct target areas: front, middle, and right (the Sunday pin!). And so the strategy here is all about identifying a specific landing area, determining the yardage, and selecting the right club. There is no room for indecision, no bailout. Total commitment through the ball to the finish is vital.

say you're facing a tough bunker shot—picture your favorite pro stepping in and splashing the ball onto the green . . . and see it roll right up to the hole to finish close (or why not IN!). Then step into his shoes and act as if you *are* that player, and make the *same* swing, the one you have just pictured in your mind. Turn those images of success into your own feelings of a good sand shot—you may surprise yourself in the process.

Battling that little voice inside your head is one of golf's greatest challenges. Negative chatter ruins more scores than anything else, so you simply have to learn

to turn the tables and fuel your performance with a more positive energy. Above all, you have to eliminate the "don't syndrome," thoughts such as *"Don't slice it out of bounds"; "Don't leave this putt short"; "Don't make a mess of this shot in front of the clubhouse window."* If that's your internal soundtrack, then don't be surprised if you slice it out of bounds, leave a putt short, or mess up in front of the clubhouse. The only way forward is to deal in direct, positive affirmations and crystal-clear visuals. Ask yourself on each shot what you want to achieve, what is your *intention*—say, to

A MASTER OF MAGIC:
The great Seve Ballesteros, pure inspiration to all.

hit a drive down the left side of a fairway, or to hole a 15-foot putt—and then focus on what you need to do to make that happen. "See" the ball flying to a specific target down the left side of the fairway; "see" the putt tracking down the line into the hole. And if you doubt your ability to hit a certain shot, don't hesitate to call in a reserve—Jack, Arnold, Gary, Johnny, Seve, Tiger, Rory, even yours truly. There's always someone on hand to help solve a problem.

A CHALLENGE FROM SIR HENRY COTTON

NOT LONG AFTER I turned professional, in 1976, I was one of a handful of promising young players invited down to Portugal to spend some time with Henry Cotton at his club, Penina. It was a golden opportunity to learn from one of Britain's greatest golfers, and one of the practice games he suggested to me that week has always stuck in my mind. The notion was simple: Over nine holes, you play an individual 2-ball scramble, but *play the worst ball every time*. So you hit two drives at the first hole, disregard your best effort and play two second shots from wherever the worst drive finished. And so it goes on. This is actually a very tough challenge, especially when it comes to holing out, because no matter how close you hit your approach to the pin, you have to hole the putt *twice* for it to count! I loved this drill and used it regularly throughout my career. Rather than just playing a casual nine holes when you next get the opportunity, go out and play your own 2-ball scramble, and see what sort of score you can put together.

PUT YOURSELF IN THEIR SHOES

SUMMER EXCURSIONS to the Open Championship with my dad were some of the best days I remember as a kid. We went first to Royal Troon in 1973, and then again to Royal Lytham in '74. In those days, you could walk right up to the ropes and get close to the players. I remember seeing Arnold Palmer, Jack Nicklaus, Tom Weiskopf, Gary Player, Lee Trevino, and Johnny Miller. I would memorize the idiosyncrasies in their swings, and couldn't wait to get back to the range at Welwyn Garden City and try to hit the shots that I'd watched them play. Out on the course I'd set up a challenge match—me and Jack versus Arnold. Or, me and Gary versus Lee. As long as there were no members around to spoil my fun, I'd play three balls on the course, picturing each player in my mind and then trying to copy them. Jack would hit a high fade, Arnold a low draw, Lee a slice, Gary a hook. Tom Weiskopf kept a very straight left arm at address. Johnny Miller's waggle went up and down toward his belt buckle. Unbeknownst to me at the time, the psychology of mimicking is incredibly powerful as a means of internalizing feelings and learning new skills. All of the positives go straight into the memory bank. I would imagine there was a gallery watching and put myself under a bit of pressure to hit the shots that I was visualizing in my mind.

I often recall these memories when I'm coaching players who are having difficulty mastering a certain shot. Of course, they often talk themselves out of it before we get to the ball: *"I'm never going to hit this shot, never have, never will…"* If that's a familiar refrain, then ask yourself a simple question the next time you're playing and face that particular shot: If you can't play it, who would you like to play it for you? Let's

**VIDEO LESSON:
THE KEYS TO CONSISTENCY**

Think *knees, turn,* and
tempo for a solid strike.

MUIRFIELD: 18th HOLE

What can you say about the closing hole at one of the
world's greatest championship links? The 473-yard 18th at
Muirfield is simply one of the classic fours in golf, a hole that
demands a solid drive before testing your nerve with one
final iron shot to a well-bunkered green—a mid to long iron
nailed at the clubhouse windows. My victories in the Open
Championships of 1987 and '92 hinged on making a four—
and on both occasions my swing thoughts revolved around
finding the balance and tempo that would give me the strike.

ST ANDREWS OLD COURSE: 14th HOLE

The Old Course was laid out by Mother Nature, and yet it is one of the most strategic golf courses on the planet. A new back tee has stretched the 14th hole to 618 yards, and with an out-of-bounds wall running all the way down the right-hand side of the fairway, this is a par 5 that gets your attention on the tee—and one that demands a good drive. The key is to pick out a specific target (perhaps a steeple away in the distance), trust in your pre-shot routine, and swing to your target. That was always my reminder on this tee shot: *Swing to the target*. The rewards are worth it. With your ball in the fairway, you can drink in this view all the way to the town, across wispy fescues and rippling mounds to the skyline of St Andrews and the R&A Clubhouse. For me, it's the greatest view in all of golf. Pure links Heaven.

STAY IN THE HERE AND NOW, AND ALWAYS PLAY TO THE PICTURE

THINKING TOO FAR ahead is a common mistake in golf. We're all guilty from time to time—there will be a "bogey hole" you think about long before you get there, a shot you're not keen on taking on. Sometimes it's a testimony to the quality of the course you're playing. Take Augusta National, for example. Often my mind would wander ahead to the par-3 12th long before I reached that devilish little hole. What club will it be today? How strong are the gusts swirling about in Amen Corner? The same thing can hap-

pen at TPC Sawgrass, where the island-green 17th hole is always a factor in the back of your mind. It's stating the obvious to say a round of golf consists of 18 holes, and that they're all important. But if you can learn to play one hole at a time, you'll score better and better. You need that mental resilience to focus on playing one shot, and one hole, at a time.

Every now and then I would complete a round of golf and have no idea what I'd scored. That's the ultimate mental state. I only wish it happened more often! But amateurs have usually calculated that they need to finish with three straight pars to break 80, or to shoot their career low score. They lose sight of the task at hand, their focus is broken, and they make mistakes. As soon as you start rehearsing the winner's speech, you're in trouble. If you really want to win, stay in the here and now. The best players in the world are the players who have the discipline to hit a shot and forget it. They make birdies, and move on. Tour players use various mental techniques to help them maintain focus, and talking to Rory McIlroy following his U.S. Open victory in 2011, I was fascinated to hear about a game he calls Super 6, in which he splits the round into six mini-games of three holes. The key then is to play each set of three holes as well as you can, and then start a new

game afresh with the next three, and so on. This sort of technique is a powerful one, as it taps into a phenomenon the human brain likes, which is the idea of "starting again." When you play Super 6, or any similar type of mind game, you're constantly giving yourself a fresh start, and it moves you in the direction of being able to play one hole at a time.

One more thought here. I've hit a lot of pressure shots in my career during the latter stages of a tournament, but I've never once stepped up to the ball without first rehearsing a certain swing thought or feeling that I wanted to achieve with an *exact* practice swing. Golf gives you the unique opportunity to make a rehearsal swing before every shot. If you picture the shot in detail and then make a halfhearted prac- tice swing, your brain will be confused—the physical action doesn't match the image in your mind. So take this opportunity to affirm positive thoughts and feelings with a real practice swing. *Make it count*. Run through what I call a "101 Shot Plan": *See it . . .* the flight and the result; *Feel it . . .* make a real full practice swing to match the shot you've pictured (the mind doesn't know the dif- ference between a practice swing and a real swing!); *Commit to it . . .* how closely can you mirror that rehearsal swing all the way to a balanced finish?

WHEN THE BALL IS ABOVE YOUR FEET …

THE ONLY PLACE you can expect to find a level lie is on the tee. After that, it's in the hands of the golfing gods. You can hit a great drive down the middle of a fairway only to find your ball sitting in a divot. On another hole you can find an awkward lie with the ball above or below the level of your feet. You need to be versatile.

As a rule of thumb, I choke down on the grip any time I find my ball off a level lie. That always enhances my sense of control and feel for the clubhead. Then I make the necessary adjustments in my stance to maintain good balance in the swing. That's the key. If the ball is above your feet, then naturally you'll need to stand a little more upright than normal. Spread your weight evenly between your feet, and play the ball in the middle of your stance. Accept the fact that your swing is destined to be fairly flat and rounded (as illustrated here in a sequence of images from

the original 1995 *A Swing for Life*). As a result, the ball will want to turn from right to left through the air, so take that into account when you visualize the shot. Aim both your body and your clubface to the right of your intended target, and then focus on swinging with balance and rhythm.

Here's a trick the more experienced player might try. If I ever need to neutralize the slope (that is, to impart a counterspin in order to keep the ball flying relatively straight), I focus on trying to get the heel of the club to the ball first, ahead of the toe. That's my swing thought. In other words, with the ball above my feet, I try to "hold off" the release, with the hint of a cutting action, keeping my left hand and left forearm firm through the ball, and finish lower than normal.

. . . AND BELOW YOUR FEET

THROUGHOUT THIS book, I've stressed the role of the knees in the golf swing, and here is no exception. Any time the ball is below your feet—and this is generally regarded as the tougher of these two shots—your knees hold the answer. As you set up to the ball, use them as shock absorbers, and build a stable stance and posture that enables you to rotate your upper body in balance. Spread your feet a little wider than usual, then flex your knees until your spine is set at a relatively normal angle. As you lean forward, stick out your rear and feel your weight on the balls of your feet. This time you can expect your swing to be a little more upright than it would be on a level lie, causing the ball to fly with left-to-right spin. Adjust your aim accordingly, and try to make a relaxed, smooth swing. The left-to-right shape will cost you distance, so club up and swing easy. Experiment with the positioning of your feet. Your follow-through will be restricted (by the slope), so find a stance that enables you to swing to a nicely balanced finish.

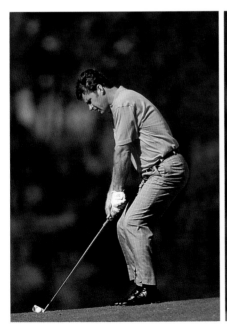

HOW TO CONTROL YOUR GAME IN THE WIND

I HAVE ALWAYS ENJOYED traditional links golf. I relish the challenge of controlling the ball in an ever-changing sea breeze. I regard that as being the ultimate test of a player's skill and artistry. And the effect the wind has on the length and trajectory of your shots playing links golf never ceases to amaze me. Yardages do become almost irrelevant. I hit my 7-iron about 160 yards in calm conditions. On a links, against even a moderate headwind, I might need a 5-iron to achieve that same distance. To thrive in these conditions, you clearly have to be prepared to think outside the box—with the imagination to visualize an array of different shots that enable you to "cheat" the wind and, where possible, use it to your best advantage. As far as shot-making is concerned, my first rule for hitting into any sort of breeze is to assess the trajectory of the shot required to get the ball to its destination. For me, that rules club selection. If I feel the only way to keep the ball down to match the trajectory of the shot I see in my mind is to use a 3-iron, even though it's only 160 yards, then it's a 3-iron! Learning to "chip" a long iron is a must for those days when the wind is up. I talked about this briefly in Chapter 5 with the "bunt" technique, and the "less is more" approach really is key to solid ball-striking from tee to green when you're playing into the wind. When you swing the club smoothly, you strike the ball more solidly and your shots fly with a lower and more penetrating trajectory, so you minimize the effects of the wind on the ball.

Guard against any tendency to quicken your swing or hit down in the wind. Your natural composure is vulnerable on a tough weather day, so try to think in terms of maintaining good rhythm in a level and balanced swing. One of my key thoughts during Open Championship week was always to focus on holding my follow-through position rock-solid, right through the bag from driver to putter, which breeds a solid action through the ball. I stress: *Good balance is vital.*

YOU GOTTA LOVE THE LINKS!
For me, the ultimate test of ball control, patience, and imagination.

Be aggressive around the green, too. A headwind multiplies any backspin and makes the ball stop more quickly than normal, so again, club up and be bold on the runners. Where you might ordinarily use, say, a 9-iron on a chip-and-run shot, I'd be inclined to drop down to an 8- or even a 7-iron into a headwind. Keep the ball down, and it'll work for you.

Though it's not as threatening as a headwind, think clearly about your strategy when a tailwind pushes you along. Your tee shots stand to benefit the most. A high 3-wood will often sail as far as a well-struck driver. The ball hangs in the air longer. Remember, in a downwind, you have to consider trouble that ordinarily would be out of reach. Particularly on links courses, where the fairways tend to be much faster, hazards that may be 300-plus yards away are feasibly in reach with the wind in your sails.

THE KEY IS always to refer to your yardage book to identify a safe landing distance, then choose your club accordingly. Look at the par 4s closely and identify trouble spots and landing zones. In a severe

wind, it may be that a rescue club or a long iron is the better option, enabling you to take advantage of the wind and play a positional shot into the fairway. Think one step ahead. Where would you most like to be playing your *next* shot from? That's the only question that matters when it comes to course management. Playing a moderate length par 4, you may not want to get too close to the green. The first hole on the Old Course at St Andrews provides a great example of this strategy. Although the fairway is about as generous as you will ever find in championship golf, most players prefer to take an iron club off the tee to leave themselves a full pitch shot over the burn.

A tailwind also makes it difficult to hold the ball on a green. No matter how much backspin you think you put on the ball, the wind will deny it, so try to land your shots on the front edge, or even short of the green. You have to factor a bounce forward into the equation; work with the subtle banks and contours that exist and feed the ball toward the hole. There are no set rules, particularly where a links course is involved, so widen your target area.

Working the ball in a cross-

IN FULL FLOW, full focus, 1990 British Open, St Andrews.

wind is a skill you can develop only with practice. Don't expect too much too soon. Shaping the trajectory of your shots with intentional spin, as we discussed in Chapter 5, is an advanced technique, and until you're capable of such control you must allow for the wind. Off the tee or from the fairway, when a crosswind threatens, the key is to aim off to the left or right, and focus on a specific target. Pick out a distinct landmark on the horizon and commit yourself to swinging and releasing the club *on that line*. It's a bit like dealing with a breaking putt—your job is to pick your intermediate target and hit a straight shot, then let the wind do the rest. And remember, any ball that rides the wind flies farther and runs a little more willingly than it would normally. So think hard before you pull a club out of your bag.

MY KEYS TO WINNING MATCH PLAY

THE EXCITEMENT AND sheer drama we witness in the biennial Ryder Cup matches is no accident. Amateur golfers around the world will testify that match play is the purest format of all, and whether that be in foursomes, fourballs, or singles, I also love the cut and thrust of it all. It really is one hole at a time, one shot at a time—the ultimate "stay in the moment" discipline. Where do you want your drive to go? How close to the pin can you hit your second or third shot? If you miss your target, can you chip it in or hole a bunker shot? If not, *this* putt has to be holed either for a half or for a win. There isn't time to think of anything else. You simply enjoy the challenge of picturing (and executing) the shots that get the ball into the hole as soon as possible! I guess one day someone will beat my record of 11 consecutive matches and the most individual points won in Ryder Cup history. Until then, here are some of my thoughts on how to pursue a winning strategy.

The importance of a fast start: Getting off to a solid start is key, and one way to do this is to use your time on the range beforehand to hit the shots you know you're going to need over the opening few holes. I can remember at Valderrama in 1997 working specifically on 8-iron, 9-iron, and wedge shots on the range because three of the first five holes featured approach shots of this distance. You knock one in close early on, and you send a message: I'm ready and I mean business. Give yourself every opportunity to grab the lead. Don't be sloppy. Miss a green with a short iron, take five, and think: "Oh, that's *okay*, it doesn't matter. I'll get it back in a minute." If you give the other guy a chance to get his nose in front and find his rhythm, it's always tough to claw back, especially over 18 holes.

Body language sends a signal: A lot has been made about my ability to intimidate opponents with physical presence, which I guess is true to an extent when you're 6 foot 4 inches in your spikes. But the real intimidation in match play is getting on with the job at hand and appearing to be totally in control of your game, your strategy, and your emotions. This is reflected (and reinforced) by a positive body posture that makes the other player believe you are 100 percent in control of the situation. Thinking back over my 11 Ryder Cup appearances, I played my best match play golf when I played fairly quickly. Tee it up, see the shot, and boom! It's up the middle. Your swing is in a groove, so there's no need to faff around. You get on with it. Your opponent thinks: "This guy knows what he's doing, I can't see him hitting a bad shot....." Now you've got him. You knock in a putt and stride to the next tee. Tee it up and whack it down the middle. It's relentless, and you set the pace.

Be in control of your emotions: If you're one of those players who blow up and outwardly give away signs that an opponent is in your head, don't be surprised if you lose more games than you win. You have to put on your "game face" or "performance face" and be prepared for whatever gets thrown at you. If you're churning on the inside, do your utmost not to show it on the outside. Show some emotion on the odd bad shot, but leave it there as quickly as you can; never show an opponent that you're beating yourself up or talking your way into a negative spiral outburst. The front nine in any match is important. If your opponent is having a great day, you need to hang on and not panic. If you find yourself three down after five or six holes, don't

go for suicide shots on 7, 8, and 9. You risk throwing the whole match away. Chip away at your opponent and don't give away any "cheap" holes. You get one back and think, "Hey, two down's not so bad after all with eight to play." Then you get another one back, and suddenly it's game on. The thing about match play is that it can all change so quickly—that's what makes it so exciting to watch. And as you begin to claw away and take back a hole or two, the momentum swings. Suddenly your opponent starts thinking: "Uh-oh, I was three up a minute ago, now it's only one...."

The psychology is fascinating. Peter Oosterhuis (now my fellow CBS Sports analyst) and I were

three down after nine holes at Lytham in my first-ever Ryder Cup in 1977, and we won 2&1. He came to me after the match and said, "Did you think we were going to lose?" and I said, "No, I always thought we were going to win." Match play is never over until it's over. If your opponents are having a good run, fair enough. You just have to hang tough, keep on giving yourself opportunities, and believe in your ability to win.

Reputation counts for nothing: The first rule of match play is, never be surprised by anything your opponent does. If you're playing someone with a reputation as a big hitter, don't panic if he stands up and booms drive after drive down the fairway. If you face someone with a reputation as a good putter, don't be surprised if he reels off three 20-footers, one after another. You must expect that these things will happen. You have to be prepared for it. Never be surprised when your opponent chips in or holes it from 60 feet ... or hits it out of bounds and is still in the hole when you get to the green. You've still got to do your own thing, play your own game. If you're shocked and wasting emotional energy reacting to what an opponent has done, it's very tough to maintain your own rhythm and routine.

Do you play the course or your opponent? Pros tend to have the confidence in their game to play

A RYDER CUP debut in 1977 at Royal Lytham, celebrated with a foursomes victory in the company of Peter Oosterhuis.

the shot they want to play regardless of what the opposition does. It's almost a mental thing—when someone opens the door a little, you rip one down the middle and stamp your authority on the hole. Most pros would go that way, and try to bury you when you've made a mistake. In the later stages of a match, you may do things a little differently. Say it's late in the match and your opponent hits a tee shot out of bounds; then you may stop and think and change your game plan. The smart shot is simply to keep the ball in play, so you choose your shot accordingly. For amateurs, the mental challenges can be the hardest to overcome. If your opponent hits one out of bounds, suddenly the amateur sees himself following suit. That's why it's difficult playing with guys who are playing badly—you see things you don't want to see. So the first important thing is to clear that negative picture out of your mind. Don't stand there telling yourself: *"Don't hit it in the trees, don't hit it in the trees…"* Because that's exactly what will happen. You have to decide what you want to do and what you're most comfortable with. If you feel good with your driver, hit the driver. The secret is to give yourself just five seconds and think the shot through until

you have a clear picture in mind of where you want the shot to finish. After you've won a hole, bank it and don't give anything away. Start again fresh.

Getting your shot in first: I was never known as a particularly long hitter, and that suited me just fine in match play. I've always enjoyed firing in approach shots before the opponent gets to his ball. I think it's true to say that I'd always rather play the second shot first, whether I'm hitting a 6-iron to his 9-iron. Being first to play focuses you into analyzing how much risk you need to take, and if you can pull off the shot you want, you immediately put pressure back on your opponent, especially if you then stand watching with your putter casually tucked under your arm. Always a nice touch.

Club down under pressure and be aggressive: Match play is a good time to be aggressive. Especially in the closing stages. You need some nervous energy. You'll hit more bad shots if you try to throttle back. So when you're between clubs, take the shorter club and make a full swing. Amateurs make more bad shots by hitting half shots. You'll quit on it—even pros do that.

Play to your strengths: My up-and-down at Oak Hill in 1995 was a classic match-play situation: I was all square playing the last hole in my match with Curtis Strange. I drove it into the rough

off the tee, but kept everything under control and told myself to play to my strengths: Wedge it to my favorite pitching yardage for the best chance of getting up and down for a four. I've never felt pressure like I did standing over that 93-yard shot with a 53-degree wedge in my hands, but I was confident I could make the shot because I had practiced it a thousand times before. This is the key to winning golf: Play to your strengths.

You have to want to tough it out: We're all going to make mistakes, but you have to keep at it. You learn that from certain players. They're always in it. Jack Nicklaus is the greatest example I have ever seen. He always wanted the chance. I always think that if you have a nasty little four-footer for a par, and the other guy is putting for birdie to win the hole, you have to want to have the opportunity to make that putt. If you're half hoping he makes it so you don't have to face yours (because you think you might miss), then your mind-set is all wrong. You really have to want it. That's the mark of the guys who play tough and win matches.

Gimmes? Simple. If you think he's going to hole it, give it. If you think they may miss, make them putt it!

ACKNOWLEDGMENTS

FINDING YOUR *Swing for Life* is a very individual process, but updating this book took a special team of people.

First, it gave me the opportunity to share some time and more than a few laughs with golf's greatest photographer, my friend David Cannon. Not only has he captured so many of the iconic images of golf's greatest courses over decades, but we grew up together in this game. He took all the photos for the original book and was here to capture all these images of the "time-enhanced" me. Now, that is art!

I also worked again with Richard Simmons, the cofounder and Editor of *Golf International* magazine. It was Richard who properly punctuated my thoughts for the original *A Swing for Life,* and Richard who sorted it all again. My job in television has given me new appreciation for finding the right words at the right time, and Richard is certainly skilled in assembling the many thoughts on the swing that run continuously through my head and turning those ideas into prose.

While my original team remained original, the book business, as we all know, has changed tremendously, and today you not only write a book but also pretty much produce a television show for electronic versions and lessons on the go. For that, I reached out to Brandt "Pacman" Packer. I have known Brandt since my earliest television experiences at ABC, CBS, and Golf Channel, where he is now stationed. He gets me, and more importantly, he gets me through in one take. He has a great sense of the game and a great sense of humor. Thanks to Brandt and his team for providing the electronics!

The Faldo Institute by Marriott once again hosted us with the perfect photographic setting, perfect facilities for instruction, and perfect hospitality for this project. Fifteen years ago, Steve Bradley brought me to the great team at Marriott, and together we created the Faldo Institute. Today it is Bill Nault, vice president of golf at Marriott International, who runs the show. I spend many days there in Orlando with master club fitter Randall Doucette, senior golf instructor Dave Dolengowski, and certified golf instructors Justin Blazer and David Graham. I'm quite proud of the experience we've built with Marriott and Marriott Vacation Clubs. Take a swing by someday.

Then there is my team from the Kingdom at TaylorMade. Mark King is an innovative and creative CEO who has built simply the best golf company in the world. The technology still fascinates me and gets my own creative wheels spinning. It's a special environment at TaylorMade. SVP and GM David Abeles and Sean Toulan, EVP of product creation, are among my favorite professionals to work with in golf. The TaylorMade team supplied the latest and greatest for this *A Swing for Life*, and they remain among my biggest supporters in growing golf, and opportunity through golf, around the world. In addition, they love this game enough to enjoy every step of the process, and that inspires all of us.

After a lifetime in a very individual sport, I am now a member of two pretty big teams in my new world of television. Often asked whether I miss playing on tour, I can honestly answer that I am quite happy in my seat in the television tower. Sure, if I could sprinkle fairy dust and play with the accuracy and consistency with which I once played, you might see me out there more, but I consider myself very lucky to have the seat I have, play the role I now play, and work with the great professionals at CBS Sports and Golf Channel. The truth is, it was Frank Chirkinian's CBS Sports pictures of The Masters that first inspired me at thirteen years old to take up golf. It is an amazing circle of life.

With the permission of CBS CEO Leslie Moonves, the chairman of CBS Sports, Sean McManus, and coordinating producer Lance Barrow, I get the chair right next to the great American storyteller Jim Nantz each week. From there, I witness the amazing antics of David Feherty and Gary McCord, the swing analysis of guru Peter Kostis, and the well-mannered Aussie-isms of major champion Ian Baker-Finch. Trust me, it is every bit as much fun as you would imagine.

In your life, have you ever worked with a pro like Verne Lundquist or Bill Macatee or my old Ryder Cup mate Peter Oosterhuis? It's a laugh, a learning experience, and a luxury to remain so close to this game, to contribute a little entertainment and to be allowed to give a little perspective to the walk inside the ropes. The on-air gang known to the TV audience is supported by associate producer Jim Rickoff and director Steve Milton leading the greatest cast of characters (whom I affectionately and respectfully call "the workers"), who bring to viewers the most glorious pictures through their tireless talent each week. From our team in the 18th tower, Gavin "Ricky" Blaine, Tommy Spencer, Kevin McHale, Kyle Carbray, and Jeff Shapter, to Hall of Fame cameraman on the ground, Davey Finch, there are so many to thank at the network. So to CBS, I want to thank you . . . let me get this straight this time . . . from the bottom of my heart.

Mike McCarley is the energetic and creative head of Golf Channel, who as the leader of this division of Brian Roberts' Comcast is bringing a new look and 24/7 exposure to our sport. With the corporate support of Mark Lazarus, John Litner, Tommy Roy, Jack Graham, and Golf Channel's new executive producer, Molly Solomon, I am part of a new media era for golf. I'm grateful for the friendship and talents of Kelly Tilghman, Terry Gannon, Rich Lerner, Steve Sands, Frank Nobilo, Brandel Chamblee, Jerry Foltz, and Gary Williams, among so many others, who make all this work so much fun.

I rely on a solid team of professionals in my Windsor office to keep it all running. Claire Hawthorne, Jason Smythe, Tom Phillips, Andrew Haggar, Gareth Williams, and my own coach,

Keith Woods, are the people behind Faldo Enterprises around the world.

There is also LeslieAnne Wade. She believed in this book and in me and never gives up. She visualizes something special and makes it happen. Thanks for lots and lots, LA.

Finally, there is my family. My little daughter Emma, who is nine years old, is my dancer, a dressage girl in training, and her only interest in a book on golf instruction is that somehow she sees her name in it. So here it is, my poppet. I'd like to thank Emma Scarlet and her big sisters and brother, who make the next swing endlessly exciting for me.

I have such admiration for the independence of my oldest daughter, Natalie, who has made her way from England all the way to L.A. to pursue her dreams in television/movie production. She is brave and smart and focused.

My son Matthew is a recent university grad who is my best friend, favorite caddie, and golf partner. He is the most well liked guy I know. After doing great work for the next generation of champions on the Faldo Series, he promises to turn all his natural charm and education into a sports biz/marketing career. I'd buy whatever he is selling.

Finally, there is Georgia. She's the smart one on the Faldo family team, an ambitious student with her own sense of self and style. Georgia teaches us lots with her passion and persistence as she studies hard with ambitions for a career in law. She'll be a formidable opponent in a legal tussle, and she's a sweet laugh for Daddy, too.

And I'd like to give a nod to my parents, Joyce and George Faldo. They were with me when I first raised my hand and said I'd like to give golf a try, and they are with me now. It's been a pretty special gift to have them to share all this with for all these years.

I've enjoyed this process with the team at Atria; the boss and a golfer herself, Judith Curr, and Sarah Durand kept us on the right path to publication.

Golf is a lifetime sport, and that's okay with me. Hope this book helps you swing easy— for life.